THE COMPLETE
JAPANESE CHIN

Pamela Cross Stern
& Tom Mather

Ringpress Books

RINGPRESS

Published by Ringpress Books Ltd,
POBox 8, Lydney, Gloucestershire GL15 6YD

Discounts available for bulk orders
Contact the Special Sales Manager at
the above address. Telephone 01594 563800

First Published 1997
© 1997 RINGPRESS BOOKS
PAMELA CROSS STERN & TOM MATHER

ISBN 1 86054 027 9

Manufactured in Singapore

10 9 8 7 6 5 4 3 2 1

*C*ONTENTS

This snapshot of Lilian (fondly known as Mab) and Ed Davis, together with some of their Gorsedene Japanese Chins, brings back a host of happy memories. They enjoyed a long and happy life with their dogs – and they shared their dogs with us. We owe them a tremendous amount for their help, advice and the benefit of their vast knowledge, which was always readily available and willingly given. As an appreciation, we dedicate this book to them.

Acknowledgements

We are very grateful to the following organisations and individuals for all their help with research, the loan of old documents, books, artwork and very precious photographs:
The American Kennel Club, The Canadian Kennel Club, The Japanese Kennel Club Inc., The Gibraltar Kennel Club, The Swiss Kennel Club, The Kennel Club Library, Kennel Union of South Africa, Mrs Carla Molineri, President Portuguese Kennel Club, Mrs Steffi Kitschbichler, Kennel Club of Austria, Mme Suzanne Dereu, Miss Maja Carlson, Sweden. Artwork, Miss Sara Forster. Artwork, Mr Stig Ahlberg, Sweden, Miss Eva Bjarlund, Sweden, Mr David Roche, Australia, Mrs Barbara Burrows (Thomas Fall), Miss Desiree Scott, Mrs Sheila Tarry, Mrs Dorothy Garlick, Mrs Ann Francis, Mrs Kath Botting, Mrs Jean Brittain, Mrs Margaret Journeaux, Mr Marc Henrie, Mr Richard Hall, Miss Anne Roslin Williams, Mrs Zena Thorn Andrews, and Mr Brian Conn, MRCVS, without whose patience and encouragement this book would never have seen life. Finally, a special thank-you to Haki, Rono and Zara, the three little Japs who patiently sat and watched it all being written!

1 ORIGINS OF THE JAPANESE CHIN

The Japanese Chin is one of the most ancient breeds of dog. Although its exact history is difficult to determine, being shrouded in the mists of time, there are plenty of indications that the progenitors of the breed can be traced back to the dogs which arrived in Japan as esteemed gifts from both China and Korea over 1,100 years ago.

ORIGIN OF THE BREED
Evidence exists that, at the end of the first century A.D., the Chinese had a type of dog known as 'Pai', which authorities on canine breeds say was a very small, short-headed and short-legged dog. Collier, writing in *Dogs of China and Japan*, states: "It has been suggested that the Japanese toy-dog, whose importation to Japan dates from the seventh century, indicates the nature of the 'Pekingese' breed of that period. This argument, however, must not be given undue weight, for there has been much communication between the Chinese and Japanese courts at subsequent periods. It is quite possible that the modern Japanese spaniel has varied from the black and white Pekingese, common in Peking, only within recent years."

In 1867, Dr W. Lockhart wrote that "a small black and white, long-legged, pug-nosed, prominent-eyed dog was one of the two kinds of Pug in China. It has been remarked that the Japanese is more apt than the Pekingese to breed true."

Collier tells us that there is little doubt that the Japanese race of small dogs originated from China. Trade and association between the two nations date back as far as the fifth century and, during the period of Tien Wu Ti (A.D. 673-686) and Ch'ih T'ung Ti (A.D. 690-696), both Korea and China constantly presented small pet dogs to Japan.

There are various theories about the origin of the breed itself. Oral history suggests these dogs may have come from Korea, and that a Korean prince went to Japan taking gifts for the Mikado in A.D. 732. These gifts included tiny dogs with flat noses. They were called Shoku-Ken and differed from the dogs in Japan at that time, which were of Spitz type.

Another theory is that, as early as 520 A.D., Bhuddist monks took Shoku-Ken from China to Japan when they went to preach as missionaries. These dogs were said to symbolise the sacred Lion of Buddha.

Others subscribed to the story of the Imperial Ch'in, which supposedly originated in China, and was owned only by Chinese royalty. It was said the last Empress of China kept 50 of these dogs in the throne room. When she entered, it was said they would line up from door to throne, standing on their hind legs and bowing until she was seated. This sounds like a nice bit of mythology to me, largely because Japanese Chins are not, in my opinion, the easiest dogs to train. The thought of 50 of them doing this in perfect unison, even for the Empress of China, is too much to believe!

The breed in its homeland.

The Chinese Imperial Ch'in was supposed to be closely related to the Chinese Temple Dog and the Japanese Spaniel, both of which were classified as Ch'ins and were also related to the Pekingese and Chow.

One story tells of a lady who owned several types of Ch'ins reporting that the Imperial (called the duck-footed Ch'in because of the peculiarly-shaped front feet) was the most regal, sensitive, intelligent and also the most demanding. The description goes on to say how slowly the Imperial Ch'in moves and adds that "coming from Peking, he withstands cold." I am afraid that the last sentence was the final straw for me and I decided that, combined with the description of the feet, it meant the writer must have had a drop too much saki, thereby confusing the Chin with a Peking duck!

Joking aside, it is reasonable to assume that, in the very beginning, Japanese Chins as we now know them were an Oriental breed. In the early days in Japan they were treated as something very valuable and precious, and were only owned by people of nobility or very high rank. This is borne out by travellers to Japan in the 19th and 20th centuries who have been able to research the Japanese Chin's origins and talk to people knowledgeable about the breed. As in many historical areas, information has been passed down from generation to generation.

DERIVATION OF THE NAME

Although we talk about the 'Japanese Chin', as we have seen, there is no real proof that its native land is Japan. Since the breed was known until relatively recently as the 'Japanese' or 'Japanese

Spaniel', we must dispel the idea that 'Chin' is original. In fact, when *The Chin Dog in Japan* was written, in the early 1960s, by Mr Koichi Uoi, Dr Hideo Wakui and Dr Seikoh Yoshida, they added a disclaimer about the name. These authors stated: "The Chin is heretofore called 'Japanese Spaniel' in Europe and America, but the term must be a mistranslation, because the Chin is neither of Spanish line, nor a hound. Taking the opportunity of pubishing this book, we propose you call it 'Chin'."

This could be as good an explanation as any of how the name originated. I received a copy of this book from the Japan Kennel Club Inc. and I feel that there has been a further mis-translation and that "Spanish line" should read "spaniel."

CONTACT WITH THE WEST

In *Dogs of China and Japan*, Collier also stresses that, in all probability, specimens of the 'Japanese' race of dogs reached Europe in the 16th century. England's trade with Japan started in 1549, and it was customary for gifts to be exchanged. In 1614, Captain John Saris was employed by the East India Company to open up trade with Japan and was received in a very friendly manner by certain of the Japanese feudal lords. Captain Saris recommended sending a "mastife, a watter spaniell and a fine grayhound" to the son of the Daimio of Hirado." The minutes of the East India Company for 1615 provide further evidence of the exchange of gifts: "Cloths to be provided for Surat, Persia and Japan; also sword-blades, knives and fowling pieces. Things considered to be sent as presents; two mastiffs, little 'Island doggs', greyhounds, etc."

Many writers have advanced the theory that the Oriental race of Toy dogs is among the antecedents of our present-day Toy spaniels. Alicia Pennington's book *Royal Toy Spaniels* contains the following extract: "In 1613, Captain Saris is reported to have returned from Japan with small spaniels in an exchange of gifts and letters from the Emperor. The writer remarks on a similarity in size, shape and colour between the toy spaniels of the Eastern and Western Courts."

Lady Mary Forwood writing in *The Cavalier King Charles Spaniel* states: "Earlier than this (1667) the Japanese Spaniel had been introduced into England. In 1613 Captain Saris returned from Japan with dogs for the King as a present from the Emperor. These were most likely the Japanese Spaniel, and Catherine of Braganza could also have brought some over because both the Dutch and Portuguese had contact with Japan."

The historian Kaempfer, who visited Japan in 1691 for the Dutch East India Company, tells us: "Since the now reigning Emperor (Kin-Sen, 1687) came to the throne, there are more dogs bred in Japan than, perhaps, in any one country whatever, and than there were before, even in this Empire."

COMMERCIAL AND IMPERIAL GIFTS

Richard Cocks, Chief Factor for Japan of the East India Company, kept a diary of events in the English company's factory at Firando, from 1615 for eight years through to the time of the expulsion of the British. He complains about the enormous number of presents required to smooth the path of commerce.

The custom of presenting dogs as Imperial gifts persisted in Japan right through to the mid-19th century. By then, Japan was perceived as a factor of real importance to the USA. Her harbours and reported coal deposits lay on the main route from San Francisco to Shanghai. Contact with the English-speaking world had ended with the withdrawal of the East India Company's Japanese trading base in 1623.

In 1852, it was announced that a new American expedition would visit the previously hostile country of Japan under the command of Commodore Matthew Calbraith Perry. At the same time, a squadron headed by Putiatin was sent from Russia with orders to watch out for Russian interests and ensure that Russia had a voice in any future developments.

Perry anchored off the coast of Japan on July 8th 1853. The complete list of gifts for presentation to his Japanese hosts makes impressive reading. It included:
One quarter-size miniature steam engine, track, tender and car.
One Francis' copper lifeboat.
One surf boat of copper.
Audubon's Birds, in nine vols.
Natural History of the State of New York, sixteen vols.
Silver-topped dressing case.
Quarter-cask of Madeira.
Barrel of whisky.
Telescope and stand in box.
Flowered silk embroidered dress.

Six dozen assorted perfumery.

These gifts, together with a missive from President Millard Fillmore, were delivered with great ceremony on July 14th. The Japanese were delighted by the generosity of the Americans, but it is recorded that the visitors were less than impressed by their Japanese gifts: "A poor display, not worth over a thousand dollars some thought."

A VOYAGE ACROSS THE OCEAN
It is believed that among the Japanese gifts were seven Japanese Chins. Four were given to the Commodore as a gift for the President, but William Speiden, the fleet purser's son, was also given a Chin. A further two were taken back to America aboard a separate ship. Thus, five Japanese Chins were taken on board Perry's own vessel. Three are reported to have died en route, while two were later transferred to the British Admiral Stirling's ship, later to be presented to Queen Victoria. The two remaining Japanese Chins reached New York safely, and were given to Mrs Augusta Belmont, Perry's daughter. Augusta Belmont became President of the American Kennel Club in 1888. Captain JC Perry's written record, *The United States Japan Expedition,* tells us that: "The Commodore, upon subsequent inquiry, learned that there are three articles which in Japan, as he understood, always form

FACING PAGE: The Japanese Chin on postage stamps, illustrating how this charming Toy breed now has worldwide appeal.
Top line (left to right) North Korea 1977, North Korea 1994; State of Oman 1970.
Middle line (left to right): North Korea 1994, Bulgaria 1991, Madagascar 1991, Nicaragua 1987. Bottom line (left to right): Tanzania 1994, North Korea 1991, North Korea 1990. *Courtesy: Paul Keevil.*

part of an Imperial present. These are rice, dried fish and dogs. Some also said that charcoal was always included. Why these should have been selected, and what they particularly symbolize, he did not learn. The charcoal was not omitted in the gifts on this occasion, and four small dogs of a rare breed were sent to the President as part of the Emperor's gift. We have observed also in the public prints that two were put on board Admiral Stirling's ship for Her Majesty of England.

"The fact that dogs are always part of a royal Japanese present suggested to the Commodore the thought that one species of spaniel now in England may be traced to a Japanese origin. In 1613, when Captain Saris returned from Japan to England, he carried to the King a letter from the Emperor, and presents in return for those which had been sent to him by His Majesty of England. Dogs probably formed part of the gifts and thus may have introduced into the kingdom the Japanese breed. At any rate, there is a breed in England which is hard to distinguish from the Japanese dog. The species sent as a present by the Emperor is by no means common even in Japan. It is never seen running about the streets or following its master on walks, and the Commodore understood they were costly."

It seems likely that Putiatin's delegation also took the breed back to Russia. To this day, the Japanese Chin has a staunch following in that country, attracting many entries at their shows. In fact, we also know of exports from Russia to Scandinavia which may, in the future, prove to be a valuable outcross for the breed.

AFTERMATH OF THE PERRY EXPEDITION

James Watson's *The Dog Book* (1906) carries an account of the fate of some of the dogs given to the Perry expedition: "Mr William Speiden, a government official in the New York custom house, is one of the few who went on that expedition who are still with us to tell the story of what they can remember of incidents of the expedition. Mr Speiden's father was the fleet purser, and the close intercourse between him and Commodore Perry was reflected in the treatment of the son, who had many privileges extended to him by the Commodore. Mr Speiden kept a diary and was good enough to give from it the following interesting information:

'In return for the large number of presents which we gave the Emperor from the President, a number were made in return, besides which Commodore Perry and others received presents from the Emperor and also from the Commissioners. Among the President's presents were four dogs of the pug character but with beautiful long hair, black and white in colour. The Commodore gave two of these dogs to Admiral Stirling of the British Navy to take to the Queen of England. The other two were named Master Sam Spooner and Madame Yeddo, and were put on board the steam frigate *Mississippi,* together with some Japanese cats. Quite a pretty little dog was given me, which I named Simoda, that being the town where I received it shortly before sailing on October 1st 1854 for home. In January of the following year and just before we reached Valparaiso, Sam Spooner died and in February Madame Yeddo also died. My pet survived them about a month. All three were buried at sea in sailor fashion, being put in shotted canvas bags. These dogs were all of the most delicate build and had to be handled carefully.

'Two other dogs came home on another ship and were sent by the Commodore for his daughter, Mrs August Belmont. We were given to understand that the dogs we received were very rare in Japan and very valuable. They were never allowed to run in the streets, but were carried in beautiful straw baskets when they were taken out of doors. Many had really attractive faces, almost human, especially in the females.'"

An enquiry from the author of *The Dog Book* to Mr August Belmont (presumably the son of Mrs Belmont) produced the following reply: "I recall the spaniels perfectly; the dog's name was Yiddo and he was black and white, the bitch was tan and white and if I remember rightly we called her Jap. They were much the same as the dogs of the present day, but as I remember Yiddo, he did not stand over so much ground as those I have seen at the bench shows, and he was a little more on the leg. I was about five years old at the time, but I have no recollection of their having any puppies, or, if they did, they did not live."

WRITTEN ACCOUNTS OF THE JAPANESE CHIN

The fact that the Japanese Chin was held in such high esteem was to the breed's great advantage. Griffis, writing in *Corea: the Hermit Nation* (1882), tells us that, "in Japan, dogs are held in very little honour except the 'chin' or Japanese Spaniel." This would concur with the earlier views of Robert Fortune.

Fortune was an eminent botanist, traveller and writer, who visited Japan in 1860. He wrote: "The street dogs appear to be the same breed as the common Chinese dog, and both have probably sprung from the same stock. On a warm summer afternoon these animals may be seen lying at full length in the public highway, apparently sound asleep; it was not unusual for our attendants to whip and kick them out of our road in a most unceremonious way. On many of them, the marks of the sharp sword of the *yakoneens* were plainly visible, and everything tended to show that, if the dogs were regarded as sacred by some, the feeling fails to secure them from being cruelly ill-treated by the common people. It was not unusual to meet with wretched specimens in a half-starved condition and covered with loathsome disease."

Robert Fortune also recorded his views of the Japanese 'sleeve dog': "The lap-dogs of the country are highly prized both by natives and by foreigners. They are small – some not more than nine or ten inches in length. They are remarkable for their snub noses and sunken eyes, and are certainly more curious than beautiful. They are carefully bred; they command high prices even amongst the Japanese; and are dwarfed, it is said, by the use of saki – a spirit to which their owners are particularly partial."

These statements are confirmed by the influential writer, traveller and teacher Lafcadio Hearn (1850-1904) who wrote: "the condition of the Japanese dog is one thing which tells powerfully against beliefs about the influence of Buddhism upon the treatment of animals."

Britain's first diplomatic representative in Japan was Sir Rutherford Alcock, a former army surgeon. Here, he describes the "ruffian" element of the population: "The Samourai, or Yaconin, moves in a very ungainly fashion, the hilts of his two swords at least a foot in advance of his person, very handy, to all appearance, for an enemy's grasp. One is a heavy two-handed weapon, pointed and as sharp as a razor; the other short, like a Roman sword and religiously kept in the same serviceable state. In the use of these, he is no mean adept. He seldom strikes a second thrust with the shorter weapon, but strikes home at a single thrust, as was fatally proved at a later period; while with the longer weapon he severs a limb at a blow. Such a fellow is a man to whom all peace loving subjects and prudent people habitually give as wide a berth as they can! Often drunk and always insolent, he is to be met with in the quarters of the town where the tea-houses most abound; or returning about dusk, from his day's debauch, with a red and bloated face, and not over steady on his legs, the terror of all the unarmed population and street dogs. Happy for the former when he is content with trying the edge of a new sword on the quadrupeds; and many a poor crippled animal is to be seen limping about slashed over the back, or with more hideous evidences of brutality."

Sir Rutherford has also left for posterity his account of the "fancy" dogs of Japan: "And first, I am to find a pair of well-bred Japanese dogs, 'with eyes like saucers, no nose, and white and tan if possible, and two years old.' My dogs are chosen, a species of Charles the Second spaniel intensified; – and, by the bye, there is so much genuine likeness that I think it probable the merry monarch was indebted to his marriage with a Portuguese princess for the original race of spaniels, as well as her dower of Bombay."

Rawdon B. Lee in his book *History and Description of the Modern Dog,* published in 1899, tells us that the notion of stunting a dog's growth through the administration of alcohol is "quite fallacious as is the belief, at one time common with us, that our diminutive toys were made so by potions of gin given at stated periods."

2 BACKGROUND TO THE MODERN JAPANESE CHIN

Dog fanciers in the West became enthusiastic about the Japanese Spaniel, nowadays called the Japanese Chin, from the mid-19th century onwards. Royal patronage and the explosion of interest in all things oriental established the breed in the eyes of British society, although no record has been found concerning the outcome of the two Chins sent to Queen Victoria. However, the continuation of trade with Japan by both the USA and Britain meant that many specimens of the breed now found their way to the West.

EARLIEST SHOWS

Rawdon Lee, writing in 1899, tells us that at one of the very earliest British dog shows – held in Holborn in 1862 – a class was provided for Japanese. There were nine entries and the class was won by Mr C. Keller's black and white dog, Caro.

Miss Elizabeth Brown of Bayswater, London, was an early breeder and owner

Miss Brown of Bayswater, London, was one of the earliest recorded owners of the breed. Pictured here is her homebred Teso. Both parents were imported from Japan.

(although, as far as we can tell, she never exhibited). Her involvement with the breed started in 1870 when her first dogs arrived in England. Chin Chin 1 and Wee Woo were described as "unsurpassable for their tininess, lustre of eye or silkiness of coat." In Japanese terms, "they had butterfly heads, sacred-vulture feathered feet and chrysanthemum tails." They lived to nine years of age and left Miss Brown with one Chin daughter, Lady Dorothea.

MING SENG

Theo Marples, the founder of *Our Dogs,* was one of the very first Englishmen to own and exhibit the breed. In 1879 he wrote: "A Japanese gentleman, now residing at Blackburn, heard of my Japanese Pug and, on seeing it, to satisfy a friend of mine, favoured me with the following communication.

**Rose Hill Mills, Blackburn,
19th September, 1879.**

"I have seen Mr Marple's Japanese Pug, and I, being a native of Japan, can testify to its being a very good one; in fact, I have seen scores in my native country, and I do not remember ever seeing a better. They are mostly black and white in colour, and in coat, size, and general conformation, I should say the little dog Ming Seng is a correct representation.

(Signed) Yamanobe Takeo,
Tokio, Japan.

Ming Seng was reputed to have been imported with a cargo of tea! He was black and white, with a protruding tongue, and, according to Theo Marples, weighed nine lbs – although other, less charitable, devotees of the breed claim he was 12 lbs in weight. The Revd G.F. Hodgson, who was acknowledged as an authority on the breed, gave Ming Seng the Gold Medal at Crystal Palace for the 'Best Foreign Dog' while he was in the new ownership of G.H. Wilkinson. Poor old Ming Seng was then sold again to Mr H.C. Joplin from Liverpool, who was later to become a member of the Kennel Club. The first recorded prize winner that we can find in the breed is Captain Anderson's The Japanese Rose. She was a prize winner at the 1865 Islington Dog Show in London. Although the UK Kennel Club has recently regulated the duration of Championship Shows, limiting all but Crufts to three days, lengthy shows were obviously not an issue in the last century. This show commenced on Friday, June 2nd and closed on Tuesday, June 6th! Hugh Dalziel's 1888 treatise, *British Dogs,* reproduces some interesting information supplied by Theo Marples: "Mr G.W. Allen won the silver medal at the Kennel Club's Summer Show in 1878 in the class for small sized foreign dogs, with Shantung, a black and white specimen, possessing the same characteristics as Ming Seng, but a little larger, being about 14 lbs in weight. The Revd. G.F. Hodgson won at Birmingham in 1873, with a light red and white Japanese Pug, the parents of which were imported by a friend of his in the 1st Dragoon Guards, who obtained them from the Summer Palace of the Emperor of China. This dog was of the same type as Shantung, an excellent specimen."

Dalziel's response to this revelation that a Japanese Pug should have come via China is noteworthy: "The dogs described by Mr Marples are certainly more like our Toy Spaniels than our Pugs;

and one – Mr Allen's Shantung – is not a Japanese, but a Chinese, dog. Mr Taunton tells me that there is a breed of Chinese small Toy Spaniels very much like the Japanese Spaniel, and that he has seen several specimens of them. In the New York Dog Show, 1880, at which I acted as one of the judges, there was a class of nine entries named Japanese Spaniels, a very equal lot, and of the same character as Mr Marples' Ming Seng."

EARLY AMERICAN DOGS
According to Andrew de Peisco and J. Johnson in *Canine Lexicon* : "Imports to the US began during later decades of the 19th century." The AKC's *Complete Dog Book* confirms that Commodore Perry, who had been presented with some Japanese Chins in 1853, in turn, presented Queen Victoria with a pair. Further specimens were sent as gifts to America, and other Japanese Chins gravitated to the USA as a result of thieving within Japanese kennels. Ships then took the stolen dogs all over the world. Two of the very first recorded imports went to August Belmont of New York. A few Japanese Chins were entered in the New York Show of 1877, and ten entered in the same event in 1882. Edd Embry Bivin, in his chapter on the Toy Group from *AKC World of Pure Bred Dogs,* published in 1983, says that Kurt Unkelbac, author of *The American Dog Book*, contended that the Chin arrived in the USA from Japan before it went to England. Mr Bivin goes on to say that the breed was first registered with the AKC in 1888.

THE FIRST US SHOW
According to the AKC, the breed was first recognised at the New York Bench Show under the auspices of Westminster Kennel Club on March 8th, 9th and 10th 1877. As can be seen in the catalogue for that show, there were certainly three Japanese Spaniels entered. It is interesting that one was imported from Japan, and the sire and dam of one of the others were also Japanese imports. It would appear that Dr Gardener's exhibit, the progeny of imported parents, was the baby in the class, being a mere nine months old. Other prize winners were more mature at two and four years of age. Unfortunately, further information does not appear to exist. However, Ch. Nanki Poo is listed in the AKC Stud Book 1888, and is regarded as the first American Champion of the breed.

ROYAL PATRONAGE
The breed in Britain by the turn of the century had a large and influential following. Alexandra, Princess of Wales, the doyenne of London society, kept a large number of Japanese Chins and her devotion to animals was legendary. She was said to be "ludicrously" devoted to dogs and it would seem that her animals were also devoted to her. A particular favourite was Joss, who accompanied the Royal party to Victoria Station on their departure to Russia. Joss objected to being left behind and when the train started, as the Princess was leaning out of the window waving, he slipped his lead and ran off along the platform in pursuit. Joss chased the train along the line, much to the horror of the watching crowd. To this day, preserved among the Royal Archives, is a telegram confirming that Joss was recovered safely!

HM Queen Alexandra with two of her Japanese Chin.

HIGH SOCIETY

Victorian and Edwardian society embraced the now-respectable sport of pedigree dogs, and the Japanese Spaniel became de rigueur. A list of active UK devotees of the breed makes interesting reading: Sir Dighton and Lady Probyn; the Countess of Wharncliffe; the Marchioness of Anglesey; the Countess of Malmesbury; the Viscountess Curzon; the Countess of Warwick; Lady De Ramsey; Sir Bernard and Lady Samuelson; the Hon. Mrs McLaren Morrison; Mr Alfred de Rothschild; the Hon. Mrs Bagot; Lady Mosley; Sir Daniel and Lady Gooch; Lady Moor; the Hon. Walter de Rothschild and Lady Decies.

Not all of them exhibited their dogs – sometimes for fear of infection to their precious pets – but all were owners and admirers of the breed. Lady Probyn was known to have had at least four Japs, who were sent directly to her from the court of the Mikado.

Lady Probyn's quartet of Japanese Chin who were imported directly from the court of the Mikado.

A ROYAL GIFT

The Rothschild family were on intimate terms with the Prince and Princess of Wales. Edward and Alexandra were notoriously extravagant, and the Rothschilds were known to offer the young Royals sound financial advice. Alfred de Rothschild had kept Japanese Chins since 1888, and imported a considerable number of animals. His first pair of importations were considered "tiny", although reviews of his kennel state that his breeding bitches were between four lbs and five lbs. Photographs of some of his stock indicate to us that they may have been slightly heavier than this, as some of the dogs are certainly rather heavily boned.

The foundation bitch, Beauty, was the dam of Facey, who was presented to the Princess of Wales and is depicted in the celebrated painting by Sir Samuel Luke Fildes. At least three more Japanese were presented to the Princess of Wales by Mr de Rothschild, including Punchie and Marvel, who was said to be a particular pet of the Princess and would allow no other dog near her. One writer stated: "Facey is a pretty dog, but is rather large and slightly undershot. Punch is a better example, being under four pounds in weight."

DAI BUTZU II

Without doubt, the most consistent winner of his day and the breed's first UK Champion, was Dai Butzu II. Although sometimes incorrectly referred to as Dai Butzn or even Dai Butzua, his owner, Mrs Eleanor Addis, in a letter to the canine press, corrected this by explaining that he was named after the statue of the Great Buddha sited in Yokahama. Dai Butzu was imported form Japan by Mrs Loftus Allen, a dedicated owner, breeder and exhibitor, who was later credited with introducing the Pekingese to the public eye. Her husband was the master of a ship engaged in trade with the Orient, and was no doubt responsible for much of the importation of her stock, which included Dai Butzu's great rival, Oji San.

Dai Butzu, quickly secured by Mrs Addis, featured in a column entitled '*Exhibited Celebrities*' in December 1894: "Dai Butzn II … is black and white and weighs only four lbs. He is a lively, playful and affectionate little dog with a splendid

Mrs Addis with Ch. Dai Butzu II – the breed's first Champion – photographed on June 8th 1895 at the Ladies Kennel Association Show.

constitution, being the only survivor out of eight kennel companions who had distemper in a most virulent form in the winter of 1893. He was ill with it for ten weeks, but pulled through, though he was cutting his second teeth at the time – always a trying time for pups. He is a good stud dog and has sired several litters this autumn. He was imported direct from Japan and is quite a typical specimen of this quaint breed. Among the latest additions to Mrs Addis's kennels is a puppy sired by Dai Butzn II which in the experience of the owner, is as fine a specimen as she has ever seen 'either in Japan or England'."

FORMATION OF CLUBS
No separate club existed in the UK solely for Japanese fanciers, and their needs at first were catered for by the Toy Spaniel Club. It has been claimed for many years that the British Japanese Chin Club was founded in 1895, but Rawdon Lee, writing in 1899, categorically states that the club was formed in 1896. The Japanese Spaniel Club of America was founded in 1883, but became defunct. Lenora Riddle quotes 1895 as the year when the club was formed, or possibly re-formed.

FROM SPANIEL TO CHIN
An 1896 edition of the UK publication *The Ladies Kennel Journal* reveals that: "The Japanese Spaniel Members who so suddenly seceded from the Toy Spaniel Club and as promptly incorporated themselves into a new club, have done so with signal success."

The *Journal* reported that Mr Lindsay Hogg consented to become the Club's first president, while Edward Murphy of Birkenhead took over the secretarial duties, with Mr Luxmore as honorary treasurer. Dr Grindrod was entrusted to draw up a scale of points.

A General Meeting of the Japanese Spaniel Club was held at the Holland Park Show in London on June 11th 1896. The Hon. Mrs McLaren Morrison (vice president) occupied the Chair. Also present were: Lady Blanche Hozier, the Hon. Mrs Bagot, Mesdames Addis, Allen, Clare, Davies, Grindrod, Stennard-Robinson, the Misses Brown and Davies and the honorary secretary.

'Betty Barkis', writing in the *Ladies Kennel Journal* in 1896 stated: "It must be gratifying to Mr Murphy to have met with such success in forming the Japanese Spaniel Club and my hearty congratulations to him, with sincere wishes for its very prosperous career. In these days of specialism no breed required a club more than this popular little dog...."

Although at this time Edward Murphy was still the club secretary, it was the treasurer, Mr Luxmore, who applied to the Kennel Club for the registration of the title of The Japanese Spaniel Club. This was granted on April 13th 1897, and reported in the May edition of the Gazette. At this time, the club was presented with two more generous donations in the shape of the Malvern Challenge Cup, presented by Mrs Grindrod of the Malvern Kennels, for the best Japanese bred in the UK, and a Puppy Challenge Cup, presented by Mrs Hall.

In 1901, The Japanese and Other Asiatic Spaniel Association, which had been formed during 1900, petitioned the Kennel Club for division of the breed by weight, with a register for those animals under seven lbs and another for those over that weight. At the same time, they also requested that the Kennel Club should allow the Pekingese a separate register, so that they would no longer be classed as 'foreign dogs'. Later that year, a general meeting of the Association was held and Eleanor Addis was appointed secretary. She immediately proposed that the Association be amalgamated with the Japanese Spaniel Club. Her proposal was carried unanimously.

Earlier on the same day, November 21st 1901, the Japanese Spaniel Club had also held a general meeting at which Mrs Addis proposed that: "This Club should amalgamate with the Japanese and Other Asiatic Spaniel Association: the united clubs to be known as the Japanese and Pekingese Spaniel Club with the rules and points of the Japanese and Other Asiatic Spaniel Association to be adopted as the rules and points of the joint clubs. Presidents to be Lady Algernon Gordon-Lennox and the Marquis of Anglesey."

This proposal was also carried unanimously. At 4 pm, a joint meeting of the two clubs was held, and Mrs Addis was instructed to request the Kennel Club to expunge the present titles from its list of registered clubs, and register in their place the Japanese and Pekingese Spaniel Club.

By 1904, George Liddel, of London, had taken over the role of honorary secretary. A committee meeting of the club in July took the decision to allow members, at a general meeting in October, to vote for a formal split, with each breed having its own club. The members obviously agreed to this course of action, and the Japanese Chin Club

came into being in 1905.

AN INTREPID TRAVELLER
One woman in particular was involved with the JCC from its inception right through until the 1920s. The Hon. Mrs McLaren Morrison had kept a large number of Japanese for many years, and was called one of the "most critical connoisseurs of the breed" by the influential *Country Life* magazine. The daughter of Lord Pirbright, she was an intrepid traveller and imported a large number of animals, including everything from Siamese cats to Tibetan Mastiffs.

Both Mr and Mrs McLaren Morrison were keen supporters of the Kennel Club, and Mrs McLaren Morrison became a member of the Ladies Branch in 1900. They lived in some splendour in Kepwick Park, Northallerton, Yorkshire, with a London residence at Hyde Park, and were passionately interested in livestock and all things oriental. Poultry was bred for exhibition, and the couple's prizewinning silky bantams were renowned in Yorkshire.

A writer in 1898 stated: "When Mrs Morrison first showed a Jap there was practically no competition, whereas now it is extremely keen and the judging very critical. The evenness of the quality exhibited, too, is so remarkable that the question of weight, rather than points, more often decides the judges' verdict. The craze for small Japs has risen just now to extremes, and, with one or two notable exceptions, no exhibitor has so many Japs under 6lbs weight."

He continued: "At the Charity show Mrs Morrison did not show her Toys as winter showing is too risky, but in the heavy-weights of 6lb and over, she scored a great innings with that very beautifully marked and exquisitely shaped Sasaki, the little Jap that has now made two journeys to India and back, and enjoys his sea trips immensely."

Sasaki was obviously quite a celebrity, and he even warrants a special mention in the *Ladies Kennel Journal* to welcome him home after his long voyage!

Not only tiny Japs were imported though. Mrs McLaren Morrison advertised a "Jap dog, imported, over distemper, great pet, about 11 lbs in weight, 63 shillings." The Kepwick park stock was campaigned extensively, and this woman did a great deal to maintain the enthusiasm and interest of British fanciers in the Japanese Chin.

THE QUESTION OF SIZE
The fashion for a very small Japanese Chins did not find favour in all quarters. In the 1890s, Mrs Addis urged breeders to be reasonable in their desire for a tiny Jap. While recognising that smallness was a requirement for all Toy breeds, she stressed that it was only one point. The proponents of the tiny Jap used the argument that the Japanese race favoured the small animal. Mrs Addis, who had travelled extensively in the East, dismissed this theory, stating that as far as dogs about eight lbs in size were concerned: "I have tried to purchase several of that size in Japan, and usually my offers were refused and really long prices asked."

She maintained that there was ample evidence that the breed had existed in Japan for centuries, with dogs varying in size from three lbs to twelve lbs.

Another noted exhibitor, Mrs Hull, who later went on to win Best of Breed at Crufts with Daddy Jap, wrote to agree

with Mrs Addis. She greatly deprecated the craze for tiny Japs, and implored judges to take care that the useful should not be sacrificed to the ornamental. As an incentive for owners of medium-sized dogs to show their pets, she suggested that shows should schedule classes divided by weight, so that they may stand a chance of competing alongside the tinies. These, she stated, were "charming little pets, but only pets, for it would be extremely hazardous to attempt to breed from them, and the mortality amongst them only goes to prove how extremely delicate they are."

MALVERN
Dr and Mrs Grindrod's Malvern Japanese were founded around the year 1890. The couple believed that the ideal size was between five lbs and nine lbs, with the proviso that they would not buy a male under five lbs nor a female under six lbs in weight. Their dogs were exercised on the Malvern hills and took exercise whatever the weather. The Grindrods were of the firm belief that the English-bred dogs – whatever their size – were stronger than the imported stock and much more able to resist distemper.

Their dogs were nearly all named after precious stones and, from photographs we have seen, their stock was of good type and quality. At one time, they lost 13 dogs with distemper and one observer noted: "The Grindrod practice of naming pets after precious stones has brought nothing but ill luck. The superstition that it is unlucky is as old as the hills."

Their noted winners included Pearl, Topaz, Beryl, Miss Ruby, Moonstone and later New Moon of Malvern, who sired the bitch, Ch. Gekko. Mrs Grindrod continued showing the breed right up to the First World War.

A BREED FOR ENTHUSIASTS

As the new century dawned, the Japanese Spaniel's star began to wane. The perceived delicacy of the breed, no doubt aggravated by the fashion for only the tiniest of Japanese, was not in its favour. The rapid advancement of the Pekingese, which was felt to be stronger and hardier, also contributed to the decline in interest. However, four English breeders in particular continued to champion the Jap, and did much to keep the breed going.

Mrs Samuelson, later Lady Samuelson, was one woman whose interest in the breed did not diminish. Her first Japanese was acquired in 1895, and at the Aquarium show in 1896 she made an offer of 75 guineas to Mrs Allen for one her new importations. Mrs Allen was not tempted, as she had already refused higher offers elsewhere. Undaunted, Mrs Samuelson went on to found one of the top winning kennels of the early 20th century.

In 1898 her stock was described as "matchless", with her two best Japanese being Jipse and Nami Nippon. The imported Jipse went on to be the breed's first bitch Champion, gaining her title in 1900, while the imported dog, Ch. Tora of Braywick, was the first Champion in the breed to sire a Champion, Mrs Gregson's Moti. Besides the kennel of dogs maintained in England, some of Lady Samuelson's special dogs were taken over to Beaulieu on the French Riviera for the winter.

Miss Serena of Regent's Park, London, was another enthusiast who did much to promote the breed in the early years. The imported Ch. Mick Mikado gained his title in 1899 and one writer described him as the "most perfect specimen of the breed ever exhibited in this country". Mrs Addis also praised his "particularly grand

Ch. O'Toyo of Braywick. Lady Samuelson's imported bitch gained her title in 1908.

head". Sadly, like so many of his peers, he was killed by distemper in an outbreak that carried off all nine of his kennel mates. Mick Mikado was followed by Ch. Kiku of Nagoya, who weighed just a little over three lbs, and Ch. Fuji of Kobe.

Miss Serena described her "Ideal Japanese Spaniel" in great detail, and what she wrote is still pertinent nearly one hundred years later: "...he is lively and highly bred, with dainty appearance, smart, compact carriage and profuse coat. He is essentially stylish in movement, lifting his feet when walking in a most graceful manner and carrying his beautifully feathered tail, resembling a chrysanthemum, plumed over his back."

Miss Serena favoured a small Japanese Chin, although she did exhibit larger stock, and she looked forward to the time when the under-four lbs dog would be the rule rather than the exception.

The Oriental Kennel of Mrs Samuel Smith was based at Hampstead, London. It was founded in 1910 with the purchase of Yo-Sen and his dam, the six-year-old Noma, from Mrs Gregson. Both were astute purchases as Yo-Sen was an immediate success, gaining his title in 1911. Lightly marked, with a large head and the most beautifully feathered hare feet, he was much admired. Noma was then mated to Tchi of Toddington, to produce Ch. Oriental Susuki, who, it was claimed, weighed just two lbs. Mrs Smith's advertisements are intriguing as, in 1916, she claimed both to be the breeder of Yo-Sen and to have been a loyal supporter of the breed ever since its introduction into England. The Oriental affix was allowed to lapse in the early 1920s.

The Toddington dogs of Mrs Hugh Andrews were housed in some luxury in the Gloucestershire countryside. Toddington Manor was the creation of Sir Charles Barry, designer of the Houses of Parliament, and the mansion was said to be a miniature replica. The dogs lived in a thatched building which boasted all modern conveniences including central heating and ventilation, a nursery, a hospital and even a kennel kitchen!

Mrs Andrews had many big-winning dogs in Pekingese, Pugs and Japanese, but Tchi, although he carried the Toddington affix, was actually owned by Mrs Knight Gregson who also owned the bitch, Ch. Nagasaki. Tchi won two Challenge Certificates, the first at Westminster (Pet Dog Show) under Rita Mosscockle in 1910, and the second at Crystal Palace in 1911, under Mrs McLaren Morrison.

A REAL CHARACTER
Mrs Mosscockle had become enamoured of the breed after purchasing her first Japanese Chins from Alfred de Rothschild. Miss Serena's Ch. Kiku of Nagoya was added to the kennel and in 1910; General Kuroki of Braywick (imported we presume by Lady Samuelson) gained his title. After giving a CC to Tchi of Toddington, Mrs Mosscockle acquired a dog sired by him and bred by Mrs Anthony Clarke. Atsuta was made up in 1913, and he was specially noted for the length and thickness of his coat.

The incredibly-named Mrs Mosscockle was quite a character. Born Rita Sparrow, she married Mr Mosscockle, who was old enough to be her father, and lived modestly in London. When he died, she discovered that he had been a millionaire and she promptly took a suite at the

Mrs Mosscockle with Mayfair Fuji, Mayfair Mimi, Mayfair Noni, Mayfair Shoki (partially obscured), and Mayfair Chigi (on her lap).

astonishing number of Japanese dogs – some silky white, others black, all long-haired, panting, goggle-eyed and looking very decorative. Eight yappers occupied one room, while six more barked away in another. In still another small room we came upon ten additional black and white dogs! Mrs Mosscockle adores her darlings and intimately knows all twenty-four of them. Coming of good families, they have taken many kennel prizes."

The magnificent gardens contained a score of miniature mounds with headstones, which Mrs Mosscockle decorated with flowers. The house contained pictures of dogs both dead and alive, and two particularly small corpses had even been stuffed and preserved in glass cases. Rita Mosscockle bore a startling resemblance to Queen Alexandra, whom she obviously greatly admired, and was, we are told, often mistaken for her when she was being driven through Windsor.

Her Mayfair prefix can still be found behind many of today's winners, and Mrs Mosscockle was still breeding Japanese Chins in the late 1930s.

THE JAPANESE CHIN PRE-1914
The First World War approached, and interest in Japanese dogs began to wane. Registrations in the UK peaked at 168 in 1911 and 127 in 1912, then hit an all-time low of only ten during 1918. It was to be 1964 before UK registrations were once again recorded in three figures. In comparison, by 1915 the relatively new Pekingese boasted 1,309 registrations, and this figure had boomed to 5,466 by 1951.

The Canadian Kennel Club records list 1909-1910 as the year in which the first

Berkeley Hotel, while deciding how to spend the money and where she was going to live. She settled on both Clewer Park, Windsor and 26 Hertford Street, Mayfair.

Cecil Beaton, in his book *The Wandering Years,* describes Mrs Mosscockle, with whom he stayed for a weekend. It is not a very charitable account of his hostess – in fact, it is rather vitriolic! His account of her dogs makes very interesting reading: "Here were an

Japanese Spaniel was registered in Canada. The October issue of the Canadian Kennel Club Gazette in 1910 gives the registration of Reba Mikado, owned by Mrs F.R. Williams of Toronto and bred by Mrs A.A. Kingdon, England. He was black and white and at that time would have been about eight months old.

The following year, Mrs Williams purchased a bitch Reba Podo, from Miss Blanche Sutcliffe in England. This bitch was whelped in July 1909. On May 23rd and 24th 1911, the Toronto Kennel Club held a show where there was a total entry of 156 dogs. This was much lower than expected because an epidemic of distemper rather decimated the entry. The judge for Japanese Spaniels was Mr Crawford, who was also judging other Toy breeds. Reba Podo was the only Japanese Spaniel entered and was awarded a first prize. Podo repeated this success at the Canadian National Exhibition Show on September 23rd and 24th 1911, under the New York judge, Mr C.G. Hopton.

On the other side of the country, the Western Canada Kennel Club Show held on May 6-9th 1913, in Winnipeg, Manitoba, lists the only entry under Japanese Spaniels as Dr M.C. O'Brien's O'Satsuma San, who won 1st in Limit, 1st Open and 1st Provincial. There appears to be no record of where Satsuma came from. The same month Terminal City Kennel Club held a show in Vancouver BC, lasting three days. Here there was quite a substantial entry of four Japanese Spaniels with all new names entered, none apparently bearing any relation to previous winners.

THE FIRST WORLD WAR YEARS
The Anderson Manor kennel of Mrs

Gordon Gratrix was among the most influential during the Great War. Mrs Gratrix's first Champion, Anderson Manor Sume, gained her title in 1913. She was advertised as being the "most perfect of her breed, being only 2 lb. in weight." After gaining her title in Mrs Gratrix's ownership, she was sold to Mrs Mosscockle for what was described in *Our Dogs* as a "fabulous price".

The kennels were founded in 1911 at Anderson Manor, in Dorset, England. The Manor was reputed to be one of the most historic houses in Dorset and dated back to 1622. The imposing house was filled with priceless, antique furniture. Anderson Manor Tuki even had her own Chippendale bed!

Mrs Gratrix obviously favoured a smaller type of Japanese, as one advertisement claimed that the combined weight of three bitches was just nine lbs, with several dogs and bitches advertised as $2^{1}/_{2}$ lbs. In fact, Japanese Chin Club members still compete annually for the Anderson Manor Trophy, which is presented to the Top Bitch under six lbs in weight. The war years saw a change of address for the kennels, and they were eventually relocated at Ludstone Hall near Wolverhampton, a moated Jacobean mansion. Many imports found their way to Ludstone Hall. In June 1914, a team of five Japanese were imported who were all reported to be of exceptional type. Despite starting in the breed in 1911, Anderson Manor dogs were advertised by 1914 as the "famous" Japanese Spaniels. Their success was immediate, and, during the war years, ten Japanese Chins gained their titles – all of them carrying the Anderson Manor affix. All but one of them were owned by Mrs Gratrix, with

Hokusai being in the ownership of Mrs Mosscockle. During 1916, Anderson Manor stock won all the Challenge Certificates on offer and at Crufts in 1917, Jakuro and Chigi did the double.

The last Japanese Champion owned by Mrs Gratrix, before she turned her attentions to the Papillon, was Anderson Manor Cherry Blossom, an imported red and white bitch who was reputed to be ten years old when she gained her title in three shows in 1921!

WARTIME RESTRICTIONS
The Great War caused serious problems for the fancy and, by 1917, the breed had only the one set of certificates on offer. The UK Kennel Club decreed that, in an effort to save food fit for human consumption, no puppies would be registered after September 8th 1917, except those bred under a special licence obtained from the KC.

This measure was, however, not considered to be stringent enough, and the KC was forced to issue the following edict: "After the Chancellor of the Exchequer disclosed that any upturn in the number of dogs being bred may lead to the reopening of the subject of taxation, it was decided by the KC on November 28th 1917 that no further Breeding Licences will, for the present, be issued."

This ban remained in force until January 24th 1919. Somehow, the ban was circumvented, as the breed mustered 18 registrations during 1918, although there were no Championship shows after the 1917 Crufts until 1920.

MONAMIE
Another woman who had a great love for both the Japanese and the Papillon was Madame Oosterveen. Her Monamie kennel was very prominent during the 1920s, and was destined to play an important part in the development of both breeds. Founded on two imports, Nuki and Carita, the Monamie Japanese had been bred and were winners before the Great War. Madame Oosterveen was a great admirer of the stock of both Lady Samuelson and Madame D'Antonio of the St. Omer kennel. Both pre- and post-war, the kennel suffered terrible losses from distemper, and was practically eradicated in 1921.

The first really big winner was Monamie Nichette who won a CC during 1921. She carried several generations of Monamie breeding but, sadly, we can find no further mention of her after her big win and can only assume that she too was a casualty of the scourge of distemper.

Ch. Princess Wo Wo of Hove gained her title in 1923, which made her the only living Champion bitch in the breed. Wo Wo was bred by Miss Langdale and described as "a glorious little black and white, she has a lovely head, short face, expressive eyes and is as sweet and dainty a little dog one would ever wish to see, she weighs five lbs."

Wo Wo was sold by Miss Langdale to Mrs Mosscockle for the sum of £130, but she was found to be "absolutely unmanageable" and was resold to Lady Anslow, who also found she could do nothing with her. Madame Oosterveen saw her at the Kennel Club Show in 1922, brought her into condition and piloted her to her title. Mrs Mosscockle, after awarding Wo Wo a first CC in 1923, was reputed to be so impressed with the bitch that she made attempts to repurchase her. The year of 1925 saw two more Champions. Monamie Michi had been registered as Michi of Kenley by his breeder, Miss Haslock, but the KC allowed a name to be changed in those days. Michi was then mated to Miss Eileen Haig's Izanami to produce the sensational Ch. Monamie Sadie. Sadie was advertised as being a record breaker, by taking all the bitch CCs in 1925. Although she was the only bitch to gain her title that year, taking the double with her sire on four occasions, both Princess Jappy of Hove and Wee Chin Babs of Hove were also 1925 CC winners. Monamie Michimyrna became one of the breed's youngest Champions, gaining his title before the age of eight months.

HOVE

The Hove affix was registered by Miss Langdale in 1921, and during that year, the kennel made its first appearance in the KC Stud Book with Princess Hasu of Hove, a litter sister to Mrs Gratrix's Ch. Anderson Manor Yoko, who was bred by

Miss Langdale's aunt Mrs Reynolds Harris. Miss Langdale had started showing at five years of age, and went on to become one of the most influential breeders and exhibitors. At the Ladies Kennel Association show in 1922, Miss Langdale did the double under Madame Oosterveen with the two red and whites, Ch. Hokusai Nippon of Hove and Princess Mouti of Hove, who was bred by Madame D'Antonio.

The kennel suffered from an outbreak of distemper in 1924 and, although there were casualties which must have caused a setback to the breeding programme, the Hove stock continued to go from strength to strength. Princess Wo Wo of Hove had gained her title in the hands of Madame Oosterveen in 1923, while Ch. Princess Yu-ki of Hove was made up in 1924. In the same year, Prince Nanki Poo of Hove was used by Mrs Stuart Rogers to produce the wonderful sire and showdog, Mr Weejum.

Marriage in 1927 saw a change of name for Miss Langdale, who became Mrs J.H.

Ch. Toro's Boy of Hove: Sire of three Champions. Owned and bred by Mrs Hudson. Photo: Thomas Fall.

Ch. Hokusai Nippon of Hove: Gained his title in 1922.
Photo: Thomas Fall.

Hudson, and a move from Sussex to Surrey. She was noted for showing a large team of dogs at the major shows, most of her winners were homebred, and the dogs were influential studs noted for stamping their type on a variety of bitches. Ch. Toro's Boy of Hove was especially instrumental – in addition to the Champions he sired, he also produced Wee Nickko of Yevot, who went on to play an important part in the development of the Yevot kennel. Hove stock was in demand throughout the world, and exports were sent to Sweden, Germany, India, Holland, and France.

The last Champion to carry the Hove affix was Mrs Bartleet's Ch. Yo Yo of Hove. He gained his title in 1938, and was a son of Toro's Boy out of Sadie of St. Omer. Yo Yo was bred by Madame D'Antonio whose renowned St. Omer kennel was, in latter years, run in conjunction with Mrs Hudson's.

ST. OMER
Madame D'Antonio's St. Omer kennel

housed many breeds, and she had already achieved success with various dogs before turning her attention to the Japanese at the start of the century. Her first and only Champion, Tama of St. Omer, gained his title in 1913 but the St. Omer affix can still be found behind many of today's winners. It is as a breeder of quality stock, not as an exhibitor, that Madame D'Antonio should be remembered.

One advertisement carried the proud boast that all of the bitches carrying the affix St. Omer "were proved, reliable breeders and a healthier group could not be found in the whole Toy dog fancy." As late as 1935 the homebred dog, Little Tartar of St. Omer, won BOB at Crufts, while Ch. Lady Toney of Hove, bred by Mrs D'Antonio, gained her title in the hands of Mrs Hudson. Both Little Tartar and Lady Toney provided a link with another great fancier of the breed, as their dam, Sadie of St. Omer, was bred by Mrs Rita Mosscockle. Madame D'Antonio was in great demand as a judge of the breed and officiated many times. More than one

Ch. Lady Toney of Hove. Bred by Madame D'Antonio, owned by Mrs Hudson.

Photo: Thomas Fall.

Lady Tartar of St. Omer (and another): BOB Crufts 1935.

Photo: Thomas Fall.

publication commented upon the wisdom of her judgements.

MORE MEMORABLE NAMES
The first Champion to be campaigned by Mrs Stuart Rogers was Mr Weejum. A red and white, he was, at the time, the breed record holder, having won 14 CCs in six years. Not a tiny, he was compact with a large, well-cushioned head, profuse coat and well-shaped feet.

Ch. Eastwood Rover: Sire of three Champions. Owned and bred by Mrs Stuart-Rogers.   *Photo: Thomas Fall.*

He proved to be an influential stud as, among his three Champion offspring, was Mrs Stuart Rogers' Ch. Eastwood Rover, who in turn sired four Champions. Despite only campaigning one bitch to her title, Mrs Stuart Rogers was noted for the quality of her bitches. At one time, she claimed that all of her bitches had won at least one Challenge Certificate.

Mrs Stuart Rogers was a generous benefactress to the Japanese Chin Club, and the trophies she donated are still keenly competed for annually. In 1980, her daughter presented some further silverware to the club, which is greatly treasured by the lucky winners.

Mrs Samuel Smith allowed the Oriental affix to lapse in the early 1920s, but it re-emerged in 1927 when it was registered by Mrs Hope. Omi Kami was reputed to be one of the best Japanese of the 1920s. He was widely used at stud and his offspring were reported as being prized in three continents. His show career had been cut short owing to the fact that one of his eyes was marked through contracting distemper. Another early inmate of the kennel was the CC winner Nadie of Hove.

TWO BREED LEGENDS

The early 1920s mark a special place in Japanese Chin history because two ladies, both of whom were to become doyennes of the breed, started their lifelong love affairs with our oriental canines.

The Riu Gu and Yevot kennels are known throughout the world. Mrs Eileen Craufurd (nee Haig) and Miss May Tovey both became enamoured of the Japanese

Chin within a few years of each other. Their interest in the breed was unswerving and never to diminish throughout their long lives.

There was always great rivalry between the two of them. Miss Tovey believed that the Japanese Chin should be as small as possible while still retaining all the breed's characteristics, but in this belief she was opposed by Mrs Craufurd, whose main priority was soundness and not necessarily size. However, they were both gracious, and shared a common love for the breed and the Japanese Chin Club.

Pre-war Riu Gu Japanese Chins at Blairhill.

Miss Tovey's first two Champions: Miya Maru and Kio Maru. Photographed at the KC Ch. Dog Show, Crystal Palace, September 1927.

Photo: Sport & General.

RIU GU

The young Eileen Haig had seen the Japanese Chin in France and was already an experienced dog owner and breeder, having terriers and Poodles at her Scottish home, Blairhill, Rumbling Bridge. Her terriers were registered with the affix Blairhill, but in 1921 the Riu Gu affix was registered for the Japanese Chins. Contact with two leading breeders, Madame Oosterveen and Mrs Mosscockle, led to the purchase of the dog Tzanagi, who was born in September 1919, and the bitch Izanami, sired by Ch. Anderson Manor Hokusai ex Mayfair Queenie.

Izanami was mated to Madame Oosterveen's Ch. Monamie Michi to produce the important litter containing Ch. Monamie Sadie and Monamie Lelio (he gained his title overseas and was described in one publication as "a gem of the first water"). Also in the litter was Miss Haig's Shi Shi of Riu Gu and Nelly Bly of Riu Gu. Another mating to Monamie Hirano provided further foundation stock for the Riu Gu Kennel.

Our Dogs of 1923 carried the news that the popular Miss Haig was to be congratulated on her approaching marriage to Colonel G.S.D. Craufurd. He was leaving Scotland, on New Year's Day 1924, to take command of the Black Watch Royal Highland Regiment in India, and newly-married Eileen was to join him. Earlier in the year, Miss Haig had already been on a tour of India and had left the dogs in the care of her father, Captain Haig. The breeding programme had continued in her absence, and now her marriage meant that some valuable breeding stock was available. Madame Oosterveen took several bitches on breeding terms and others remained with

Captain Haig or were fostered out.

By the 1930s, a breeding programme had again been established at Blairhill and, as well as the Japanese, Dandie Dinmont Terriers and Scottish Terriers were strongly fancied. Soasano of Riu Gu, a five-lb dog sired by Ch. Eastwood Rover ex Gilly, was purchased from Mrs Stuart Rogers in order to strengthen the stud team. A repeat mating of Soasano produced the bitch Champion Ka-Zi for her breeder. Among the brood bitches, the tri-colour Tora of Riu Gu was reported to be greatly prized.

YEVOT

Miss Tovey's Yevot Japanese were her lifelong companions. As a child, she was not allowed to have a dog but, in 1923, she was presented with Kio Maru as a gift. At Crufts 1925 he won the CC and BOB, although he had to wait until 1928 to gain his title, as he was competing against the big winners Ch. Monamie Michi and Ch. Mr Weejum. Miss Tovey's success was immediate, and even before her first CC winner gained his title, his homebred daughter, Ch. Miya Maru had won hers. 1931 and 1932 saw the Yevot kennel take the double at Crufts, and 1936 saw the fabulous litter brothers, Sakura of Yevot and Haru of Yevot, gain their crowns.

Life was not always a bed of roses, though, and the ubiquitous scourges of distemper and hardpad meant many heartbreaking times for all dog breeders. Modern vaccines were unheard of, and travel to and from shows was far from simple. Miss Tovey wrote: "When chatting to Jap lovers, whose knowledge of the breed has covered many years, we talk of the Japs of our childhood. Those who first attracted our love for the breed.

Miss Tovey's red and white Ch. Ume Maru, pictured with Ember of Caytonray.

Photo: Thomas Fall.

ABOVE: Ch. Sakura of Yevot: One of the great pre-war Yevot Champions.   Photo: Thomas Fall.

LEFT: Miss Tovey's Kosen of Yevot: Dam of Haru and Sakura.

The tiny dainty Japs, so fairylike in their movement, so gay, so oriental. Little pointed feet, scarcely touching the ground. What a thrill to breed one like that again. I looked at the old pedigrees of my first Jap. Famous names of the past, old cuttings and pictures of Japs before my time, what a thrill to feel we are part of that building up. Are we preserving the picture? I met some of those famous people when I was young. Lady Sybil Montgomery left me one of her Japs when she died. She was a beauty. Unfortunately, she died with so many in my kennels from distemper. Such a nightmare then for Japs. How much we have to thank present-day medical skill for!

"In those days we had to remain at Crufts two days, up till 8 o'clock at night. In a dismal hall at Islington. On our return home we watched our Japs with dread, so often infection came back with us and death followed. Memories bring joys, also sadness, but dreams remain of the most perfect Japs we have seen and hope to see in the future. I can't tell you how many times we were wiped out. We would think our Japs were recovering and then the distemper went on in another form. From passing blood then on to the lungs and finally the brain. We are very lucky today. Our love for our Japs broke our hearts. So many gave up."

A UNION OF STOCK

Mrs Craufurd and Miss Tovey were wary of using each other's stock at stud, but others were quick to see the advantages of a union between the two strains. Erna Bartleet went on to become a post-war secretary of the Japanese Chin Club, and she had the dubious honour of campaigning and owning the last two Champions to gain their titles before

hostilities were once again resumed with Germany. Ch. Yo Yo of Hove was bred by the great breeder Madame D'Antonio, but the beautiful dog, Yoshiteru of Mikazuki, was homebred and sired by Ch. Haru of Yevot out of Yoshida of Riu Gu. Mrs Bartleet had owned Japanese Chins since the early 1930s and was among the first to reap the benefits of combining Yevot and Riu Gu stock.

THE SECOND WORLD WAR

The war years were immensely difficult for dog owners in all countries. Many breeders were called up for war service, and an uncertain future and severe rationing were not conducive to dog breeding. Miss Tovey served the Admiralty in Bath during the war, as well as managing her dogs. Bath was heavily raided in return for the attacks on Cologne, and Ivor House, Miss Tovey's beautiful Georgian home, lost its roof and windows. Luckily, both she and the dogs survived. The small meat ration was used for the dogs' breakfasts, and many an hour was spent queuing at the local

Mrs Bartleet's Ch. Yoshiteru of Mikazuki: The last pre-war Champion.

Photo: Thomas Fall.

slaughterhouse. In one of her many letters to me, Miss Tovey wrote: "We stood in long, long queues. Cows, unfit for human consumption, were sold whilst still hot. Those at the end of the queues were often unlucky. People's tempers were short at the fish shop, they often had to refuse customers and one lady picked up a fish and smacked the face of the fishmonger! Bath was a political city and we had no protection. The planes came low and shot at anyone in the street. We had 'points' for a luxury cake, but I swapped these for tinned meat which I gave to the dogs."

EARLY AKC RECORDS

Going back to AKC records for 1926, we learn that no Japanese Spaniels were registered that year. There were eight the following year; three in 1928; nine in 1929 and, in 1930, there was a tremendous leap in registrations to 130 – one wonders what provoked this? However, the phenomenal increase was not sustained and drifted down to 72 in 1931 and 67 in 1932, increasing again the following year and peaking at 121 in 1935.

There were no registrations in 1938 and only one in '39, picking up slightly in the 1940s, but with a high point of only 75 in 1942 when America joined the conflict.

JAPANESE BLOODLINES

It was not only in the UK and USA that the war years took their toll on the breed, but in Japan too, where the dog population, including Chins, suffered. After the war the Japanese imported Chins from both Britain and America to help improve their breeding stock, depleted by earthquakes and the effects of war.

Oudenarde Sugar Puff holds a special place in the history of the breed, as he was the first Japanese Chin ever to be imported into Japan from the UK. Sugar Puff became a Japanese Champion and Asiatic Champion, winning Best in Show at the International Championship Show in Tokyo. He sired winning stock in Japan, and it would be interesting to trace the pedigrees of the present-day Japanese

Gottingen Kumochi No Harutaka (dog) and Kumochi No Kozakura III of Riu Gu: The two imports discovered in Japan by Jean Brittain.

imports to see if he figures in their background. The Kumochi kennel of Ineko Shimogawa, who was born in Brooklyn, New York but returned to Japan as a child, was extremely influential. Mrs Shimogawa exported her dogs to both Britain and North America from the 1930s onwards. Kumochi-No-Chiya I was exported to Canada in 1931 and became an American Champion. Mrs Shimogawa registered her kennel name with the AKC, and the Kumochi bloodline became a valuable international commodity.

In 1965, via Jean Brittain, who lived in Japan for a time, Mrs Shimogawa supplied a Kumochi bitch puppy for Mrs Craufurd's Riu Gu line. The bitch was Kumochi No Kozakura III of Riu Gu, who was subsequently mated to Ch. Momus of Riu Gu producing two bitches and a dog. One of these bitch puppies, Niju Kokuseki No Riu Gu, was then put to the red and white dog, Toshita of Honshu to produce the fabulous Ch. O'Kayama of Riu Gu. Jean had brought home a male puppy from Mrs Shimogawa, Gottingen Kumochi No Harutaka, who was, like his sister, rather too large for top winning, but he enjoyed local show success. He was much loved as a family pet, was full of energy and life, and lived until the age of eight, when he developed a heart murmur. Mrs Craufurd told Jean Brittain that her early American imports had the Kumochi prefix in their pedigrees. As Jean says: "What an achievement for this Japanese kennel to have circumnavigated the globe!"

THE BREED FACES A CRISIS
Registration numbers for the breed began to plummet, as the horror and uncertainty facing the world began to take its grip. The Kennel Club Emergency Committee appealed to all dog owners to breed as few litters as possible. Japanese Chin registrations for 1940 totalled only 16 in the UK, and when one considers that Pekingese registrations numbered 671 and Cocker Spaniels in excess of 2,200, it is possible to judge what a perilously dangerous state the breed was in.

Mrs Craufurd, in her rural Scottish home, would have found it easier than many to keep a number of animals. Country dwellers, used to a hard life and having to make do and mend, frequently had the added advantage of having a friendly neighbouring farmer who would let them have fallen stock which could be used to feed hungry dogs.

Mrs Hope was still breeding in 1939, and her Oriental kennel was destined to play an important role in the development of the breed after the war. Mrs Wharton-Tigar was another who kept her Japanese Chins throughout the war. She had used the litter brothers, Ch. Sakura and Ch. Haru of Yevot, on her bitches in the late 1930s and was producing quality stock which promoted the Chalrose affix to full advantage.

Miss Jameson's Redcedars had been established as early as 1928 when she purchased Madame Katsiha from Miss Crouch, who was a most successful exhibitor, having campaigned two Champions, Sir Gugnunc and Chittojodan.

The Redcedars were advertised as "being noted for their fearlessness and complete lack of 'nerves'. Two large rooms in their owner's home have been turned over to the dogs completely, and they have the benefit of a large garden

Ch. Sir Gugnunc: Gained his title in 1928. Owned and bred by Miss Crouch.

Photo: Margaret Ellerman.

and a cement playground. They lead a thoroughly free and outdoor life and are as strong and hardy as any small breed." The Redcedars were destined to enjoy great post-war success and were to play an influential part in the founding of Margaret Journeaux's Navy Villas, an affix which is still very active in the breed to this day.

POST-WAR RECOVERY
Championship Shows were non-existent in Britain during the war, and keen exhibitors made do with Limited and Sanction Shows. These were often held to raise funds for patriotic causes, and huge sums were raised by dog breeders and exhibitors. With the cessation of hostilities, the Kennel Club was eager to help breeders re-establish, and members of the Japanese Chin Club were keen to start showing their beloved dogs and renew mutually beneficial international links.

RETURN OF CHAMPIONSHIP SHOWS
The first post-war Championship Show for the breed was held in London on June 13th 1946. Mrs Knapp, the Japanese Chin Club secretary, was also secretary of the Papillon Club and the Griffon Bruxellois Club. A joint show was held, comprising these three Clubs together with the Maltese Club, and Mrs Stuart Rogers judged the Chins.

The dog CC was won by Fuku of Riu Gu, and the bitch CC by the red and white, Oriental Chrysanthemum, who went on to become the breed's first post-war Champion. She was born in 1939 and was a daughter of the last dog to gain his title in 1938, Yoshiteru of Mikazuki.

The KC granted permission to hold a second Championship Show in 1946, and this took place on October 22nd in London. This time the show was held in conjunction with just the Papillon Club, and Mr T.A. Moffatt was the judge. The results were the same and Fuku won a

Fifi of Chalrose: Typical of the stock bred by Mrs Wharton-Tigar.

Photo: Thomas Fall.

Ch. Tangerine of Maywood. Owned and bred by Miss Miles.

Photo: Thomas Fall.

second CC. He was born in June 1938, and we can find no further record of his having any other wins.

VETERAN TRIUMPHS
Two more Club Championship shows took place in 1947. The first, in co-operation with the Papillon Club, was on April 23rd, and the dog CC winner was the incredible Yoshiteru, who had been born eleven years earlier. The bitch CC went to Mavis of Redcedars, one of the first major wins for her dedicated owner Constance Jameson. Mavis, when later mated to Ch. Dream of Redcedars, went on to produce the lemon and white dog, Ch. Puffin of Redcedars, who, after winning BOB at Crufts in 1950 and 1951, joined his sire at Mrs Mary Brewster's Robwood Kennel in the USA.

The second Championship Show of 1947 was held in Shepherds Bush, London. This was a joint show of the Maltese Club, Griffon Bruxellois Club, Japanese Chin Club and the Invicta Pekingese Club. Miss Tovey was the judge, and the young Dream of

Redcedars won his first CC. Mrs Golding won the bitch CC, a first as well, with the red and white, Goldfinch of Redcedars. Mr and Mrs Golding's youngest daughter, Ketha June, was the real owner of Goldfinch, and the Goldings went on to become very active members of the Japanese Chin Club. They are still remembered with affection by many senior breeders.

INFLUENTIAL FRIENDS
Mrs Bartleet's last Champion was the attractive bitch, Mignon of Maywood. She was sired by Oriental Kano out of Sprite of Maywood, and was bred by Miss Miles. Sprite was a good producer and and is behind many of the early winning Riu Gu dogs. She was of interest as she was by an untitled dog, Augustus of Gildridge, who had been bought in by Mrs Craufurd to join the Riu Gu kennel. He was born in 1942, and was basically of Hove breeding. Sprite's dam was Reni of Mayfair.

Miss Miles had trained at the Ardross kennels of Mrs Beamish Levy and was, in fact, her first pupil. She went to Mrs Mosscockle's establishment at Clewer Park as a companion and, when Mrs Mosscockle died, the Mayfair dogs were left to her. Miss Miles eventually joined Mrs Craufurd, who left Scotland for Worcestershire in 1951.

A YEVOT STAR

Miss Tovey's first post-war Champion was the red and white bitch, Kin-Sen of Yevot. Unusually, Kinney as she was known, was sired by a dog bred by Miss Tovey's great rival, Mrs Craufurd, but she carried Yevot bloodlines on both the sire and dam's side. Kinney was recruited to play the part of Henrietta in the film *The Elusive Pimpernel*, starring Margaret Leighton and David Niven. Some of the film was shot in Bath, but Kinney also made many trips to Elstree Studios where she was a great hit with the cast and crew.

Miss Tovey must have been pleased with the results of this mating as it was repeated in 1949 to produce the great winner, Ch. Kesumi of Yevot, who went

Mrs Alexander's two great Champions, the red and white Yensuki of Yevot and Mitsu of Riu Gu.

Photo: Thomas Fall.

Ch. Kesumi of Yevot: BOB Crufts 1952 and sire of Ch. Shira Tama.

Fox Photos Ltd.

Ch. Shira Tama of Yevot: Sire of Kohanna.

Ch. Kohanna of Yevot.
Photo: Thomas Fall.

on to win Reserve BIS at Bath Championship Show and a BOB at Crufts in 1952. Kesumi was not only a show dog. He produced the red and white, Ch. Yen Suki of Yevot who was owned by Mrs Alexander, and the influential Ch. Shira Tama of Yevot who gained his title in 1955, having survived an epidemic of hardpad early in 1953 which killed twenty of his kennel mates. His dam reared her litter while also suffering from hardpad. The fact that Shira Tama was spared was a blessing for the Yevots, as he sired the litter brother and sister, Chs. Aki and Chiisa (considered by many to be the best-ever Yevot bitch), and also the beautiful red and white bitch Ch. Kohana of Yevot.

A RIU GU DYNASTY
Mrs Craufurd's fortunes in the show ring increased with the move to

Worcestershire. No doubt the ease of travelling, compared with the long trips from Scotland, helped when exhibiting the Riu Gu stock. Oriental Jenny Wren was mated to Julius of Riu Gu to produce Ch. Pegasus of Riu Gu, who was the first

Mrs G. Evans' Lamtoi Yo San of Jongary, one of five Champions sired by Aquilo of Riu Gu. *Photo: Thomas Fall.*

Ch. Midas of Riu Gu.

Photo: Thomas Fall.

Ch. Momus of Riu Gu.

Photo: Thomas Fall.

of nine male Champions in direct line. Pegasus sired Perseus, who was the sire of Am. Ch. Silvius of Riu Gu of Robwood.

Before export, Silvius was mated to Persephone of Riu Gu, to produce Midas.

Through Midas, we come to the wonderful Momus, whose first CC was awarded by the late Fred Cross. From Momus came Nyorai, the sire of Yama Kaze and Yama Kiko. Yama Kaze sired Tenson Daku for Mrs Craufurd's niece Eileen Haig, and Daku, in turn, was the sire of Tenson Atae.

TRANSATLANTIC TRADE

Early in 1950, the Journeaux of Navy Villas bought Miss Jameson's Tensi of Redcedars, a black and white dog with a cobby body, profuse coat and beautifully cushioned face.

Mary Brewster of the USA's Robwood kennels had already made several notable purchases from Miss Jameson. These included Ch. Puffin and Ch. Dream of Redcedars, and, as a result of meeting Mary, Margaret Journeaux sent three bitch puppies out to the Robwood kennel. These three bitches were Yola, Yu Shee and Kume, all of Navy Villas. All three became Champions, with Yola (advertised as one of the best-ever Robwood Japanese) winning BOB at Westminster, and Yu Shee winning the Japanese Spaniel Club of America West Coast Specialty.

Several more Navy Villas puppies found their way across the Atlantic to Mary Brewster and her daughter, Sari. The Brewsters visited Jersey, and even tried to persuade Margaret and Bevan Journeaux that they should make their home in America, but they decided their future was in the Channel Islands. A trip to Southampton to deliver a puppy to Mrs Brewster, who was due to sail back home, enabled Margaret to spend some time aboard the Queen Mary.

Eileen Troger, a Chin fancier from the

Margaret Journeaux's Tensi of Redcedars. Bred by Constance Jameson.

Champions Yola, Kume and Yushee: The first Navy Villas exports to Mary Brewster in the USA. Bred by Margaret Journeaux.

USA, started corresponding with Margaret. This led to Wee Wun of Navy Villas starting a show career in America, with Eileen's son Lee as his handler. Wee Wun weighed just two lbs at six months. In Margaret's own words: "He was a darling little red and white boy and was, as far as I can remember, the biggest winner overall."

NEW BLOOD

As the 1950s drew to a close, Mrs Craufurd decided that an outcross was necessary. The American dog, Prince Shika, was imported and added much-needed new blood to the breed. He was mated to Perdita of Riu Gu to produce the second top stud dog of all time, Aquilo of Riu Gu. It was ironic that the first Champion to be sired by Aquilo should have been Miss Tovey's Ch. Yoko Tani of Yevot. He was a reluctant show dog, although he did win one CC, but he went on to sire five Champions including the fabulous group winner, Ch. Lamtoi Yo San of Jongary and Miss Kathleen Sully's first Champion, Princess Kuchi Nashi. Significantly, Aquilo is also the grandsire of the top stud, Ch. Nyorai of Riu Gu, through his dam, Quilos Dolly Dimple of Riu Gu.

Although Miss Tovey had used the slightly larger Riu Gu dogs at stud and had awarded them CCs, she still kept very firmly to her beliefs: "My great aim throughout life has been to keep the fine dainty bone Jap, typical of Japan. Whoever would expect Japan to be happy with anything coarse, the country speaks of gay glittering Geishas. The art of growing miniatures – may we keep our Japs with this uppermost in our breeding."

She used her chairman's letter in the *Club Bulletin* to exhort members to remember that Japs must be cobby with fine bone: "We must avoid the flat pike head. A round forehead and oriental eye is essential for a Jap. In so many breeds, eyes are becoming smaller."

Her advertisements in the canine press reminded readers that Japanese Chins, and particularly Yevots, were "small

Miss Sully's Ch. Princess Kuchi Nashi.

Photo: Thomas Fall.

Ch. Camplane Usui No Sadamitsu.

Photo: Thomas Fall.

gems". The difference between the two great kennels was diminishing, and *Dog World Annual* of 1958 carried an advertisement for both kennels on the same page. Miss Tovey proudly proclaimed that Ch. Mitzi of Kurraba had won three CCs, while Mrs Craufurd advertised the fact that she had a lovely litter sired by Ch. Pierre of Kurraba!

3 *CHOOSING A PUPPY*

Japanese Chins are very gay, happy little dogs, always ready for a game. They also revel in being lap dogs, and will sit quietly on your lap or curled up in a chair enjoying an evening's television. They are friendly and enthusiastic about meeting people and have many other delightful facets to their nature.

It has been said that 'chin' means cat-like, and certainly Japs do exhibit some cat-like qualities such as the way they use their paws to wash their faces. They will also hold toys, or some types of food, between their front paws.

Japanese Chins do not need to wear coats in winter. Their own fine, silky coat grows quite profuse with the advent of cold weather. However, they should not be exposed to draughts and, if they are caught in a shower of rain, will need a quick rub over with a towel to dry them off once inside. Japanese Chins are not delicate, hothouse flowers, and should not be treated as such. If you use common sense in looking after them, they will reward you with many years of pleasure and companionship.

My own involvement with the breed began when the Ladies' Kennel Association Championship Show was held at Olympia in London, which is quite a while ago. I was walking round the gallery with Nora Down – an eminent and well-respected Toy judge. We stopped at the ring where Japanese Chins were being exhibited and remarked to each other how attractive they were. I said I would love to have one. As we watched them moving round the ring, I said to Mrs Down: "They all seem to hump in the back. I wonder why?" We looked a little longer and then the answer became evident. The Chins were not wearing collars and leads but crotcheted harnesses which fastened on to a crotcheted 'lead' in the middle of their backs. It was this that gave them a most peculiar appearance! At that time it was the vogue for ladies who showed Chins to present them in this fashion.

I already owned several Toy breeds, and some months later went to mate a Griffon bitch. Lilian Davis, who owned the Gorsedene prefix, was the owner of the stud dog and well-known for the excellent dogs she bred. I saw several of her Japanese Chins – they were very beautiful, outgoing and had quite charming personalities, and I decided that I must have one of her breeding. Cheekily, I asked if I could have pick of her next litter and said I wanted a bitch. In due course the litter arrived – all boys! I was most anxious for a bitch, so asked if I could have pick of the next litter. Mrs Davis agreed and eventually Cho Cho, the start of my line in Japanese Chins, joined the rest of the Sternrocs. This was also the start of a deep and lasting friendship with 'Mab', as Mrs Davis was affectionately known. She became not only my best friend but my mentor and adviser.

However, if you are reading this before choosing your first Chin puppy, I have to say that my own fortunate experience is not necessarily the orthodox way to go about getting a pup.

MAKING THE DECISION

The decision to have a dog must be a family decision. It is not one that can be made lightly or without a great deal of thought. The dog, when you get it, will very quickly become an integral part of your family and is likely to remain so for many years.

If you decide to have a puppy, rather than an older Japanese Chin, you should not purchase one under a minimum of eight weeks of age. The puppy should be fully weaned and wormed. It is better to wait until the first injection has been administered. You will still have the pleasure of bringing up a baby. Make no mistake, acquiring your Japanese Chin puppy will be just like having a new baby in the house. It will mean regular feeding times, play times, sleep times and training times.

Anyone who tells you that a puppy is no trouble has never looked after one

properly, but the pleasure the task brings is its own reward.

PURCHASING A PUPPY

Perhaps you have seen the slogan 'Pedigree Dogs – Buy from a Breeder', and wondered why you should buy from a breeder rather than the local pet shop or puppy farm. Nowadays there are even widely-advertised dog hypermarkets which stock a myriad of breeds, can get the 'model' you want, and sell it to you on hire-purchase terms.

No reputable breeder who has the welfare of his or her dogs at heart and cares about their puppies, sells to any of these establishments. Such breeders feel it incumbent upon them to make sure the puppies they have so carefully raised are going to the right homes.

When you buy from breeders their reputations are at stake. They will offer planned puppies, whose parents have been carefully selected to try to produce the ideal puppy. The father, a stud dog, will have been carefully chosen to complement the dam, who will have had the best possible care before, during and after whelping. The puppy in question will have been reared to the highest possible standard.

If you purchase a puppy from one of the other sources you may, or may not, be told its background, but in any case you have no way of checking on what you are told. You will perhaps be given a certificate of health and told that the animal is not returnable merchandise! The breeder, on the other hand, will make sure that you know exactly how to look after and feed the puppy, and will give you the dates on which your Japanese Chin has been wormed and vaccinated. If your puppy has not been vaccinated against distemper/hepatitis/leptospirosis, the breeder will tell you to take it to your veterinary surgeon, when to have the inoculation done and what precautions to take in the meantime.

When you buy from a pet shop or puppy farm, the puppy has been bought by these 'dealers' as cheaply as possible for re-sale. The person who bred the puppy cannot care about its welfare, and when the youngster leaves the breeder for the dealer it will associate with other dogs, some of which may be diseased. In other words, the purchase of such a puppy means that you may have saved a little on the purchase price but could be in for a prolonged series of visits to the veterinary surgeon to restore the puppy to good health. This will actually cost you far more than the price you would have paid a reputable breeder.

FINDING A BREEDER
The best method of finding a breeder is to contact your national Kennel Club – every country has such an organisation which will always be pleased to supply lists of breeders. You could also ask for a list of Championship Shows and Breed Specialty Shows, then pay a few visits to take a really good look at the breed in depth. You can approach one of the exhibitors or, since addresses will be in the catalogue, get in touch with those whose dogs you like at a later stage.

Write or telephone the breeder. Do not casually drop in on them. All breeders are busy people and have a routine to follow with their dogs. Make an appointment to go to see their puppies. Breeders are usually very generous with their time and advice, provided potential owners visit

them by arrangement. Do not visit several kennels or breeders in one day without being completely honest, and saying that you have been elsewhere. Once you find a puppy you like, why keep on looking? It is not clever to keep shopping around. Infection is easily carried on the feet from one place to another. Never visit a dogs' home or rescue organisation and then go on to a breeder.

When you have explained what you are looking for, you will probably be given a choice of one or two puppies. If you are looking solely for a pet, and not a potential show dog, the breeder may well keep the show prospects to one side.

The aim of every breeder of pedigree dogs should be to breed something as close as possible to the Breed Standard as approved by the Kennel Club, as well as to improve stock, and most also strive to produce a Champion. Unfortunately, even in the best of breeding programmes, one cannot guarantee a Champion in every litter. Some puppies which have been carefully planned and reared may be lovely, but not quite up to show standard. They will make wonderful pets; there is nothing wrong with them, they are not ugly or deformed, and the pet owner who buys one is indeed fortunate in knowing he or she is purchasing a puppy raised to such a high standard.

HOW TO CHOOSE A PUPPY
There are several important factors which you should bear in mind when making your choice. Japanese Chin puppies are truly adorable. They should be outgoing, airy-fairy little characters with insatiable curiosity. Reject all thoughts of taking home the shrinking violet who hides behind a chair, will not come to you, or

sits in the corner ignoring everyone and everything – always go for the extrovert.

You are looking for a happy, healthy puppy. The body should feel firm, without ribs that stick out or a protruding tummy out of balance with the rest of the puppy. Eyes should be bright, and the little tail well up. A puppy, any puppy, should have a mixture of appeal: mischief, curiosity, sensitivity, buoyancy, playfulness, and serenity when asleep.

LOOKING FOR A SHOW PROSPECT

You get what you pay for. If you want a prospective show-type puppy, say so – such a puppy will be more expensive than the obvious pet, but buying a Japanese Chin at eight weeks of age and hoping it will be good enough to show is a gamble. The older the puppy you purchase, the more obvious the good and not-so-good points should be. Puppies do change and the ugly duckling *can* change into a swan; by the same token, the pick of the litter does not always live up to early promise and, if you really want a show prospect, it is better to buy one somewhere between five and ten months of age, which will, of course, be proportionately more expensive.

Unfortunately, when most people come into a breed, they rarely do enough research before making a purchase, and it is often a case of the heart ruling the head. Apart from the obvious, already mentioned above, you will be looking for a puppy that looks 'square' in outline, with fine bone, 'pointed' hare feet, a level topline and, if possible, a proud carriage of head. You will want the eyes to be round, large and dark and, hopefully, you may catch the characteristic "look of astonishment" where the whites of the

eyes are showing. You want a decent-sized head, not a little head with pinched, narrow jaws and dilated nostrils. The puppy will not change teeth until about five to six months of age, and some Toy breeds are notoriously slow. Do make sure the tongue is not visible, and that the bite is not crooked, that is, with one jaw at an angle to the other. The coat should be soft, silky and fluffy (not harsh or wiry) and will probably be a bit sparse on the tail. You will be looking for straight front legs, with feet that point straight forward, not in or out, and firm hindquarters that are not cowhocked, which means that the hocks point in toward each other.

COLLECTING THE PUPPY

When you go to choose or collect your puppy, only the immediate members of your family should go, ideally just one person. Do not be talked into taking friends and extra people along. It is your choice.

Reputable breeders will ask questions before selling you a puppy. Be glad breeders do so. It shows they care. They will want to know if your garden is fully-fenced and escape-proof, whether you have any very young children, and if there is someone at home most of the day – puppies need companionship.

You are entitled to ask to see the mother of the puppy, and the other whelps in the litter (even if these are not available for sale). The sire may not be available to be seen, because the owner of the bitch will usually choose a stud dog and take the bitch to the dog to be mated.

Remember to enquire about vaccinations. Most breeders will not let a puppy leave until after the first injections,

Colour is a matter of personal preference. Japanese Chin can be black and white or red and white.   *Photo: Marc Henrie.*

and they will advise you as to when the next one is due. The breeder will give you a copy of the pedigree and, if your Japanese Chin is a show-type puppy, the registration certificate from the Kennel Club.

You will also receive a written diet sheet and probably a small supply of whatever food the puppy is used to. Follow this to the letter. The breeder will advise you about increasing the size of meals and decreasing the number of times the puppy is fed.

Do not haggle or bargain over the price of your puppy. The reputable breeder spends a great deal of money on getting the right stock to breed and in feeding and caring for both parents and puppies. There is no such thing as a cheap puppy that is also well-reared and well-bred.

When you collect your Japanese Chin, remember this may well be the puppy's first outing and separation from dam and littermates. Take with you some old towels, newspapers and tissues, in case of travel sickness. It is a good idea to have a

The expert can assess show potential, and indicate where a pet home may be more suitable.
Photo: Marc Henrie.

cardboard box, or even a small travelling crate, for the puppy to travel in. Probably the best time to collect the new puppy is in the morning – this gives the pup time to get accustomed to the new surroundings before the loneliness of the night.

The puppy will soon adapt to your way of life, but there are one or two cardinal rules to be observed when your new family member first reaches your home. Of course, everyone will be anxious to see, cuddle, and play with the new baby.

But take it easy! Do not overwhelm the puppy. Your Japanese Chin is going to be with you for a long time, and everyone can have their turn during the ensuing days.

First of all, take the puppy into your kitchen. The reason for this is 'first associations'. Kitchens are usually warm, and there will always be a lingering smell of food. We figure these two things are welcoming signs to the new arrival, who may think this new place could be alright after all. If there are children in the household, please do not leave them alone with the puppy. It is only natural they will want to pick up and love the pup – but too tight a squeeze, or an untimely wriggle, and the puppy may accidentally drop to the floor. This could cause damage – and heartache. Children have to learn to respect animals, and, when this has been achieved, there is no doubt that it is a very fortunate child who has a dog as a companion.

TOYS
Your puppy, like all youngsters, will want some toys to play with. Happily, the wants of a Japanese Chin puppy will be simple. A puppy can have lots of fun with a man's sock knotted (better than tights or stockings as, usually, they are not so fine), the cardboard core of a toilet roll, and, of course, a little ball or something that rolls. These simple things will keep your puppy amused for hours.

Do beware of toys that have bells inside them. They can get dislodged from the toy and be swallowed. The same goes for 'eyes' in some toys, such as teddy bears.

A word of warning: an old sock is an ideal toy, provided that you are a tidy sort of person. However, if you are in the habit of taking clothes off and throwing them anywhere, it will be difficult for your Japanese Chin to understand what is yours and what is the puppy's!

BEDTIME
Make a point of playing – not too boisterously – with the puppy for 15 to 20 minutes before bedtime. A cardboard box lined with a snug blanket, placed on newspaper and surrounded by a playpen – still in the kitchen – is an ideal 'bedroom' for the pup. For the first night (or the

first few nights) in this new home, your puppy could well feel lonely and will let you know about these feelings of misery by little cries. Unless you wish to have your Japanese Chin sleeping with you until the end of time, make sure the puppy is warm and comfortable, then resist the urge to take your 'baby' to bed. Harden your heart and, if you have an old-fashioned alarm clock with a loud tick, put this just outside the playpen (do not forget to switch off the alarm). The puppy may feel reassured, not totally alone, and drop off to sleep.

BASIC HEALTH CARE
The Japanese Chin is a fortunate breed, in that, at present, it has no known hereditary defects – Brian Conn, MRCVS, the breed's foremost veterinary surgeon, who is also a respected owner and judge, describes Japanese Chins as healthy, hardy little dogs. After years of experience of the lines he knows best – Gorsedene, Riu Gu and Sternroc – he can confirm that most live to a happy and healthy age of ten years or more.

In the 19th century, distemper was the scourge of the breed in most countries, as with many other breeds. Since the advent of vaccinations, which are now quite sophisticated, this is now a thing of the past. Immunisation is considered a good prophylaxis, or preventive measure, and all Japanese Chins are routinely vaccinated against distemper, hepatitis and leptospirosis.

Of course, any dog, like any child, can develop some illness or other. However, it is not the norm with Japanese Chins, so it is always best to consult your vet for advice when you are not happy with the health of your dog.

Make sure that, when you go to your vet, you can describe any symptoms the Japanese Chin has: loss of appetite; when the dog last ate; if it has been drinking an abnormal amount of water; what the stools are like; and whether there is any difficulty urinating. In other words, exactly the kind of thing a doctor would ask during a consultation about your own health.

HEALTH WATCH RESEARCH
The Japanese Chin Club of America has recently compiled a Health Watch Research committee report. The premise is that prevention is better than cure, and the survey focused on health and structural conditions in the breed. Unfortunately, the actual numbers of those who were contacted and who responded are not available. It would appear, however, that the incidence of health problems recorded is, in most cases, less than ten per cent, in other words low enough to suggest that these conditions are not common and could be largely accidental in nature.

Significant findings to emerge from the survey are that the average litter size is three, and that life expectancy is twelve years for males and ten for bitches. Somewhat disheartening was the suggestion that two major problems in Japanese Chins are heart conditions and

It is a bewildering experience for a puppy when it first arrives in its new home.

Photo: Marc Henrie.

luxating (slipping) patellas. A total of 21 respondents cited heart problems and 15 luxating patellas. I emphasise that the scope of the survey is unclear. I must say that, while judging the breed in at least 13 different countries during the last eight years, I have been delighted to find that slipping patellas are the great exception, not the rule. In my opinion, the incidence of this condition seems to be diminishing.

The survey found that cataracts are mostly age-related and infrequent, and that deafness occurred in a tiny minority of Japanese Chins. It was, however, surprising to note that there was a significant number of difficult whelpings and Caesarian sections. Not quite so surprising is the preponderance of pinched nostrils – in my experience these often occur in the 'tinies' with small heads.

SUMMARY

As far as the health care of your own Japanese Chin, both as a puppy and as an adult, is concerned, I can only pass on the advice of my parents and grandparents, who were very much involved with dogs as breeders, exhibitors and judges. They always said: "Treat a puppy like a baby." Of course, if you have never had a baby, you could always read Dr Spock! Joking aside, canine health care is a matter of common sense. Unless you are an experienced breeder, avoid home remedies. Go to your veterinary surgeon for advice and, if you are worried about your Japanese Chin, go without delay.

4 GROOMING AND SHOWING

Japanese Chins, with their silky coats, are one of the easiest breeds to keep well-groomed. From six weeks old, they should become accustomed to being groomed on a table. In days gone by, many older breeders used to groom their dogs on a towel on their laps. Personally, I have never found this very satisfactory and, in my opinion, you get a better finished effect when grooming with the dog on a table.

To groom this way has added benefits if you plan to show your Japanese Chin because the puppy gets used to being on a table for a pleasant occurrence. Puppies should not associate a table with a trip to the vet, which is the excuse given by many exhibitors when their dogs misbehave or refuse to stand up for table examination at a show.

EQUIPMENT
For normal grooming a pure-bristle brush is really the best. It is quite an expensive investment, but pays dividends. Such a brush does not tear the coat, or pull it out, as a wire brush will. You will also require two steel combs – one fine-toothed and one with wider-spaced teeth.

When preparing to groom your Jap, have the grooming tools ready, together with a small tin of baby powder, cotton-wool balls and some distilled water. We also use a spray coat-dressing – alternatively you could use a mixture of bay rum and fresh rainwater.

Vigorously brush the coat in the opposite direction to the growth, starting at the tail and finishing at the head, not forgetting upward brushing on the legs and brushing well behind the ears. I can recall judging Japs a few years ago in England and my fingers wandered over the dog's head and to the back of the ears, where, on each side, I felt two huge matts of hair. I suppose I looked a bit askance at the exhibitor and said: "Oh dear!" They responded by enquiring what was the matter and I asked them to put their hands where mine were. "Oh, that's part of the ear," they told me, and were quite surprised when I demonstrated that they were in fact matts of hair.

Should you, by any chance, find a matt on your dog, liberally sprinkle it with baby powder and gently tease it apart with your finger and thumb. Then use the bristle brush alternately with your hands,

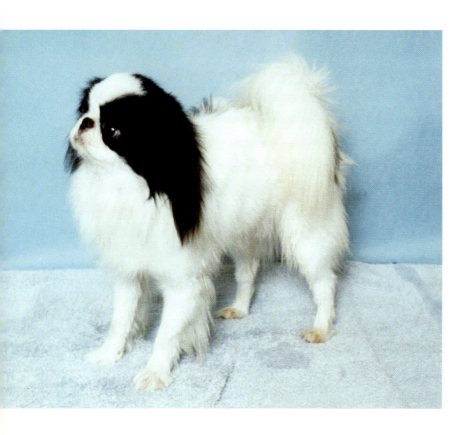

The Japanese Chin needs regular attention in order to stay in good condition.

Ears should be checked regularly, and the hair behind the ears must be combed through to prevents matts forming.

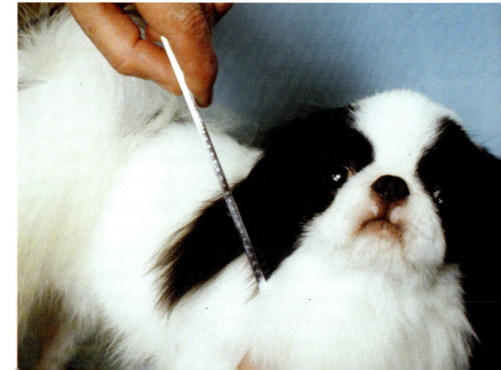

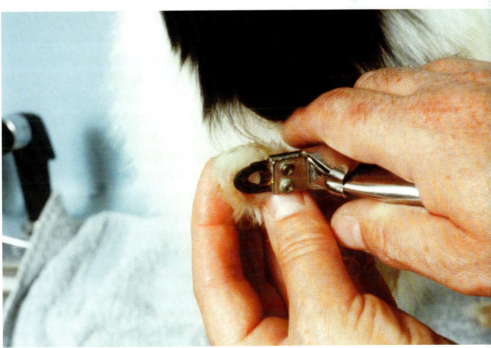

The nails may be trimmed, and this should be done using nail-clippers, making sure you do not cut into the quick.

and so on until you have got rid of the matt. This is how to remove matts with the minimum loss of hair and minimum discomfort to the dog. If you have no patience and rake it out with the comb, it could leave a bald patch and you will have a very unhappy dog who did not enjoy the pulling process.

After all the coat has been brushed in the opposite direction to growth and is matt-free, layer it a little at a time and brush back in the direction of growth. Finally, comb through with the wide-toothed comb, using the small-toothed comb on leg and ear furnishings. Then spray with one of the proprietary coat dressings.

EARS
Check the inside of the ears to make sure they are clean and free from wax or irritation. Matts behind the ears can often be caused by a dog scratching the ears, because they itch or irritate. Do not poke around in the dog's ears. If you suspect something is not right, consult your veterinary surgeon.

EYES
To make the dog feel fresh, each eye should be wiped over with a fresh cotton-wool ball soaked in sterile water.

TEETH AND FEET
Check the teeth. Then check the pads of the feet to make sure there is nothing stuck between them and that the nails are not too long.

GROOMING TIPS
Take the opportunity to stand your Japanese Chin in a show pose, talking to the dog all the time. Eventually, your dog will hold the pose without the pressure of your hands. What a clever dog! Give a pat, put the lead on, and off you both go.

It is not necessary to groom a Jap every day, in fact you could lose coat if you do. Twice a week should be sufficient, with a daily wipe over the eyes and a check to see that your dog's rear end is not dirty. If it is, baby powder and the brush come into their own again.

PREPARING FOR SHOW
Preparing your Jap for show is a little different in that the dog will need a bath, may require nails cutting and, for best results, will have to be brush- and blow-dried.

I firmly believe that good coats – length and texture – are bred for and not made, but you can make the best of what you have got. Incidentally, I know that some Japs are kept caged most of the time in an effort to grow coat, and this I deplore. Ours have always led a natural and happy life, running both on concrete and grass.

We bath our dogs in a full-size bath with a rubber mat on the bottom, and use a spray which mixes the water to the right temperature. Always, always test the temperature of the water before you wet the dog! We use an insecticidal or cream shampoo specially manufactured for dogs, mixing the shampoo in a jug before we start. We then wet the dog all over with the exception of inside the ears and are very careful not to get water or shampoo in the eyes or nose.

It is better to wet the body first and leave the head until last. Then lather the shampoo into the coat, rinse, shampoo again, rinse extremely well and partly towel dry. We work in a very small amount of human hair conditioner and

ABOVE: Before bathing your Japanese Chin, make sure you have all the equipment you need readily available. We recommend you use a pure bristle brush.

BELOW: Groom the coat thoroughly, making sure there are no tangles or mats.

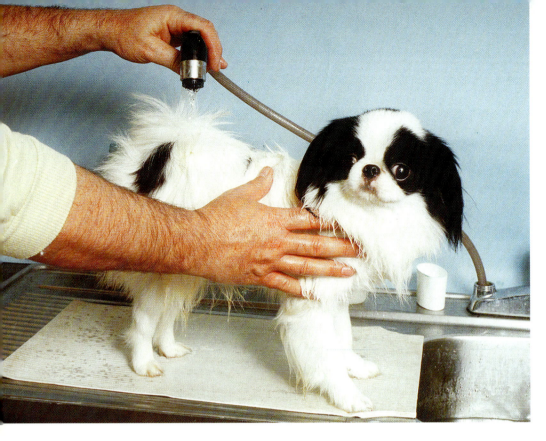

ABOVE: Wet the coat using lukewarm water.

BELOW: Apply the shampoo. This can be an insecticidal type.

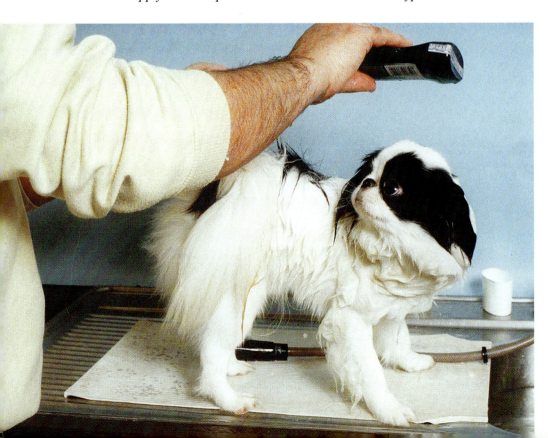

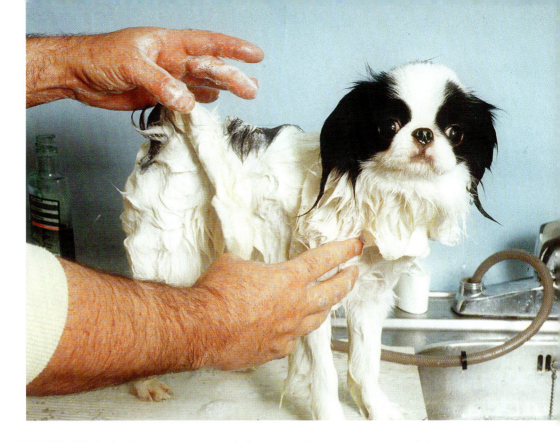

ABOVE: Work the shampoo into a rich lather, making sure you avoid the eyes and ears.

BELOW: The head can be washed, using moistened cotton-wool – again, make sure you do not get shampoo into the eyes or the ears.

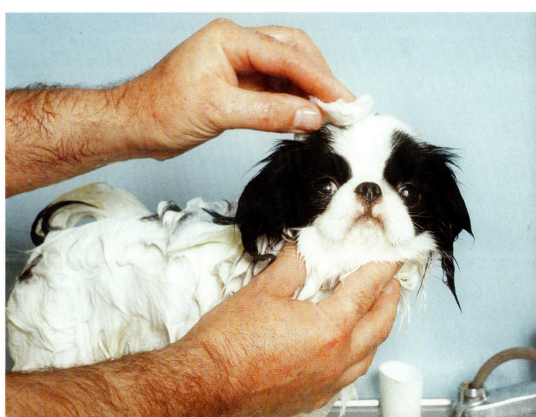

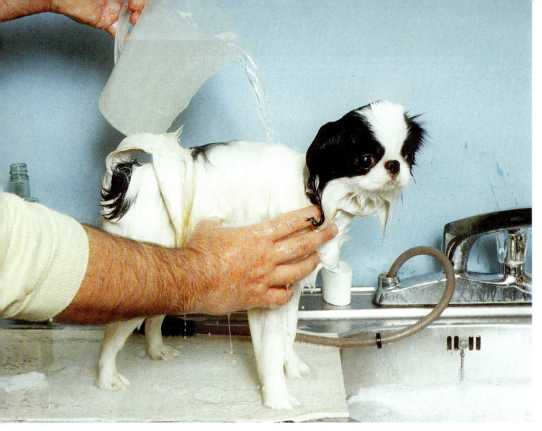

ABOVE: Rinse the coat thoroughly. At this stage you can shampoo again, and apply conditioner if you wish to do so.

BELOW: Part towel-dry the dog, making sure you do not rub the coat.

ABOVE: *A hair-dryer is the ideal way to dry the coat. Do not blow the dryer directly at the dog's face, and make sure the setting is not too high.*

BELOW: *Use the hair-dryer in one hand, and with the other hand, brush through the coat with a bristle brush.*

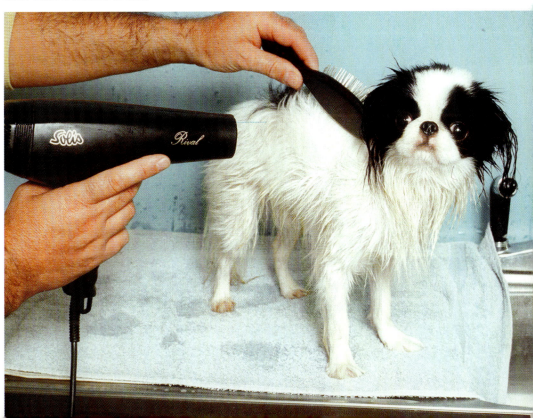

Most dogs do not object to this procedure, and will stand or sit patiently while they are being dried.

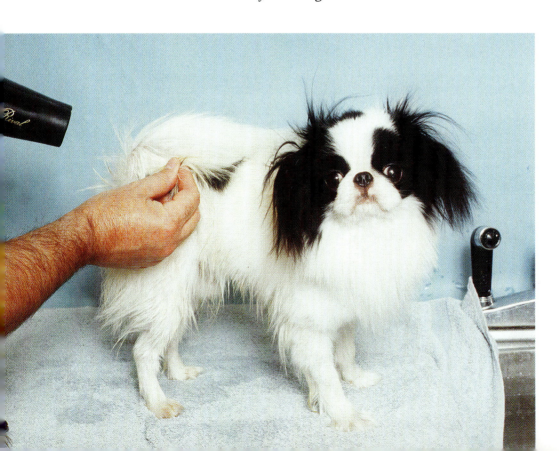

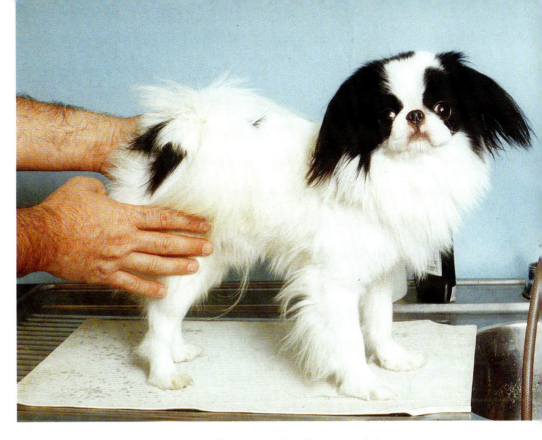

The finished result: A clean and well-groomed dog.

comb it through with a wide comb. Then we put the dog back in the bath and rinse out the conditioner absolutely thoroughly, otherwise it will clog the coat when dry. Part towel-dry the dog – squeeze the coat, do not rub it. Place the dog on the table, standing on a thick bath mat and dry with a hair-dryer, first ruffling the coat with one hand until it is just damp, then using the brush in one hand and the drier in the other.

I had one particular line of Japs – mother, sons and daughters – who were always convinced, as soon as they stood in the bath and before I even turned on the water, that I was going to drown them. These have been the only ones who insisted on really wailing while they were being bathed, just to make sure nothing untoward happened. Otherwise, you

should encounter no problems with baths.

AT THE SHOW
I have a theory that I do not want to bring back from a dog show more than I take to it – other than prize cards! What I really mean by this is avoiding fleas, ticks or disease. To this end, I have always tried to be very particular, and my show bag is packed to cope with all eventualities.

If it is a benched show (infrequent in the US), always pack (in a separate plastic bag) a cloth and diluted disinfectant. First, I wash my benches and the cage wires with this, then I place a layer of newspaper on the floor of the bench, topped with white paper and finally bedding – towels or a snug rug. We used to put curtains round the inside of the cages, too. I see no point in walking the dog round the show ground before you go into the ring – or at any time for that matter. Anything could happen. A larger dog could lunge and frighten, or even nip, your Japanese Chin. You want your dog on its toes and watching everything while you are showing, not displaying a bored 'I've seen it all before' attitude.

We always take an exercise pen to the shows with us (this is standard procedure in North America and Australia, but not always in England). We set it up with the bottom lined with newspaper – and more white paper on top in case the newsprint comes off on white dogs. We could then pop the dogs in there when we got to the show to let them have a drink and relieve themselves. This is very easy to clean up, too: all you have to do is roll up the soiled paper and dispose of it. After the show and before they go into their travelling crates to return home, the dogs all have their feet wiped with disinfectant.

FIRST SHOW FOR A PUPPY
The first time you take a puppy to a show, the most important thing of all is to make sure the puppy enjoys the occasion. Our dogs only have to see a show bag or travelling crate and they go mad with joy and anticipation.

If, at the first show, the puppy appears to have forgotten everything it has learned about walking on a lead etc., do not worry. One of my top winning bitches went to her first show and certainly was not afraid, but walked to the middle of the ring, sat down, and took it all in, refusing to budge an inch!

USING YOUR ADVANTAGES
Exhibitors in some countries are fortunate

because, when they go into the ring with their dogs, they do not have to stand in numerical order, but can stand where they choose. What an advantage this is to a clever handler! This system means that, if you have a dog who excels in movement, or if there are others in the class whose handlers move at a snail's pace, you can choose to be out in front, leading the line. On the other hand, if you have a dog that is a bit unsure, you do not want to be the first to be seen leading the parade round the ring. You prefer to be where you have a little more time to give the dog confidence – at the other end of the line, initially.

Then there are those exhibitors who are showing a rather large specimen: if they are wise, they make sure they do not accentuate the obvious by standing next to a 'tiny'. Similarly, a dog with a medium amount of coat will look better when standing next to one who is out of coat. And so it goes on – you have to keep your wits about you.

NEVER STOP SHOWING
Try to keep the dog interested and alert the whole time you are in the ring. Your Japanese Chin is there to show off and, after you have been seen by the judge, do not relax and start talking to your neighbour. Pick your dog up, or let it sit down. The clever handler knows the judge will often glance back down the line, in between looking at exhibits, especially if he has seen a dog that caught his eye. If it is in someone's arms rather than standing on its own four legs, too bad!

KEEPING THE DOG'S INTEREST
There are many ways to do this, none

better than talking to your Japanese Chin. If, when you have been going through your training exercises at home, you have taught your dog to respond to you, you have a million 'tricks' at your fingertips. When his attention is starting to wander you say "Ooh, look at that!", or "Where's the pussy cat?", or "Is that Daddy (or whoever) over there?" If your Jap has been taught to look for things, these remarks will keep the dog on the alert.

When using my dogs at stud, I always used the phrase: "Where's the nice girl?", or: "Isn't she a nice girl!" This came in useful in the ring. In a Toy Group one can usually figure out which exhibitor will pick the dog up in their arms part of the way through. If you have a keen stud dog, make sure that you stand next to an exhibitor like this. When they pick up their dog it is your cue to say to yours: "Where's the nice girl?" The exhibitor might say: "It's not a girl, it's a boy," to which I always retorted: "Please don't tell him!"

ON THE FLOOR
If you are exhibiting at an indoor show, floors are quite often wooden or slippery. It is amazing how many exhibitors wear boots or chunky shoes that make a lot of noise as they clump up and down showing their dogs. It is no wonder that some of the Toy breeds find the row off-putting. At times like this a pair of rubber-soled shoes are a boon. It always seems a shame, too, when you are showing an elegant little dog, to wear trainers. There must be another style of comfortable shoe to complement your exhibit.

AFTER THE SHOW
When you return home from the show, one of the first things you should do is remove your shoes and leave them to be disinfected. If you have puppies, it is not a bad idea to change clothes before you go into them.

It goes without saying that show dogs should have a special area where, for a day or two, they do not mix with other dogs. As soon as you can, give them a quick check to make sure they have not brought home any unwelcome 'friends' in their coat.

Dogs who have been at a show all day will have used up a certain amount of nervous energy and, on their return home after a few minutes free exercise, will appreciate perhaps some egg and milk and some specially tempting food before they drift off to sleep, dreaming their own special dreams of an exciting day.

5 THE BREED STANDARDS

I n this chapter, three offical Breed Standards for the Japanese Chin – the British Standard, the American Standard and the FCI Standard – will appear in bold type. These will be followed by my interpretation of the Kennel Club Standard and an analysis, including the points on which they differ.

THE KENNEL CLUB STANDARD

(Reprinted by kind permission of The Kennel Club, London.)

GENERAL APPEARANCE
Elegant and aristocratic, smart, compact with profuse coat.

CHARACTERISTICS
Intelligent, happy, lively little dog who has a look of astonishment, peculiar to this breed.

TEMPERAMENT
Gay, happy, gentle and good-natured.

HEAD AND SKULL
Large in proportion to size of dog, broad skull, rounded in front, and between ears, but never domed.

Nostrils large, black, except in red and whites where the colour can be appropriate to markings. Muzzle very short, wide, well cushioned, i.e. upper lips rounded on each side of nostrils, jaws level.

EYES
Large, dark, set far apart. Most desirable that white shows in the inner corners, giving characteristic look of astonishment (wrongly called squint), which should on no account be lost.

EARS
Small, set wide apart, high on head, carried slightly forward, V-shaped, well feathered.

MOUTH
Bite preferably level or slightly undershot; wry mouth or tongue showing highly undesirable.

NECK
Moderate length, carried proudly.

FOREQUARTERS
Legs straight, fine bone, giving slender

appearance, well feathered down to feet.

BODY
Square and compactly built, wide in chest, "cobby", length of body equal to height at withers.

HINDQUARTERS
Straight, viewed from behind, good turn of stifle, profusely feathered from the back of thighs.

FEET
Slender, hare-footed, feathered at tips, pointing neither in nor out.

TAIL
Set high on level back, profusely feathered, closely curved or plumed over back.

GAIT/MOVEMENT
Stylish, straight in movement, lifting the feet high when in motion, no plaiting, and showing no weakness in hind movement.

COAT
Profuse, long, soft, straight, of silky texture. Absolutely free from curl or wave, not too flat, having a tendency to stand out especially at frill of neck.

COLOUR
Black and white or red and white. Never tri-colour. Red includes all shades of sable, lemon or orange. The brighter and clearer the red the better. Colour evenly distributed on cheeks and ears and as patches on body. White should be clear, not flecked.

SIZE
Daintier the better, providing type, quality and soundness are not sacrificed. Ideal weight 1.8-3.2 kgs (4-7 lbs).

FAULTS
Any departure from the foregoing points should be considered a fault and the seriousness with which the fault should be regarded should be in exact proportion to its degree.

Note: Male animals should have two apparently normal testicles fully descended into the scrotum.

THE US STANDARD 1993
(Reprinted by kind permission of the American Kennel Club)

GENERAL APPEARANCE

The Japanese Chin is a small, well balanced, lively, aristocratic toy dog with a distinctive Oriental expression. It is light and stylish in action. The plumed tail is carried over the back, curving to either side. The coat is profuse, silky, soft and straight. The dog's outline presents a square appearance.

SIZE, PROPORTION, SUBSTANCE

Size
Ideal size is 8 inches to 11 inches at the highest point of the withers.

Proportion
Length between the sternum and the buttock is equal to the height at the withers.

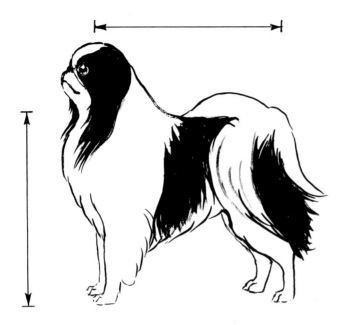

Correct proportions of the Japanese Chin.

Substance
Solidly built, compact, yet refined. Carrying good weight in proportion to height and body build.

HEAD
Expression
Bright, inquisitive, alert and intelligent. The distinctive Oriental expression is characterized by the large broad head, large wide-set eyes, short broad muzzle, ear feathering, and the evenly patterned facial markings.

Eyes
Set wide apart, large, round, dark in color, and lustrous. A small amount of white showing in the inner corners of the eyes is a breed characteristic that gives the dog a look of astonishment.

Ears
Hanging, small, V-shaped, wide apart,
set slightly below the crown of the skull. When alert, the ears are carried forward and downward. The ears are well feathered and fit into the rounded contour of the head.

Skull
Large, broad, slightly rounded between the ears but not domed. Forehead is prominent, rounding toward the nose. Wide across the level of the eyes. In profile, the forehead and muzzle touch on the same vertical plane of a right angle whose horizontal plane is the top of the skull.

Stop
Deep.

Muzzle
Short and broad with well cushioned cheeks and rounded upper lips that cover the teeth.

Nose

Very short with wide, open nostrils. Set on a level with the middle of the eyes and upturned. Nose leather is black in the black and white and in the black and white with tan points, and is self-coloured or black in the red and white.

Bite

The jaw is wide and slightly undershot. A dog with one or two missing or slightly misaligned teeth should not be severely penalized. The Japanese Chin is very sensitive to oral examination. If the dog displays any hesitancy, judges are asked to defer to the handler for presentation of the bite.

NECK, TOPLINE, BODY
Neck

Moderate in length and thickness. Well set on the shoulders enabling the dog to carry its head up proudly.

Topline

Level.

Body

Square, moderately wide in the chest with rounded ribs. Depth of rib extends to the elbow.

Tail

Set on high, carried arched up over the back and flowing to either side of the body.

FOREQUARTERS
Legs

Straight, and fine-boned, with the elbows set close to the body. Removal of dewclaws is optional.

Feet

Hare-shaped with feathering on the ends of the toes in the mature dog. Point straight ahead or very slightly outward.

HINDQUARTERS
Legs

Straight as viewed from the rear and fine boned. Moderate bend of stifle. Removal of dewclaws is optional.

Feet

Hare-shaped with feathering on the ends of the toes in the mature dog. Point straight ahead.

COAT

Abundant, straight, single, and silky. Has a resilient texture and a tendency to stand out from the body, especially on neck, shoulders, and chest areas where the hair forms a thick mane or ruff. The tail is profusely coated and forms a plume. The rump area is heavily coated and forms culottes or pants. The head and muzzle are covered with short hair except for the heavily feathered ears. The forelegs have short hair blending into profuse feathering on the back of the legs. The rear legs have the previously described culottes and in mature dogs, light feathering from hock joint to foot.

COLOR

Either black and white, red and white, or black and white with tan points. The term tan points shall include tan or red spots over each eye, inside the ears, on both cheeks, and at the anal vent area if displaying any black. The term red shall include all shades of red, orange, and lemon, and sable which includes any aforementioned shade intermingling or overlaid with black. Among the allowed colors there shall be no preference when judging. A clearly defined white muzzle and blaze are preferable to a solidly marked head. Symmetry of facial markings is preferable. The size, shape, placement or numbers of body patches is not of great importance. The white is clear of excessive ticking.

GAIT
Stylish and lively in movement. Moves straight with front and rear legs following in the same plane.

TEMPERAMENT
A sensitive and intelligent dog whose only purpose is to serve man as a companion. Responsive and affectionate with those it knows and loves but reserved with strangers or in new situations.

THE FCI STANDARD
No. 206/02.12 1992/GB
(Reprinted by kind permission of the
Fédération Cynologique Internationale)

ORIGIN
Japan.

UTILIZATION
Companion Dog.

FCI CLASSIFICATION
Group 9: Companions and Toys, Section Nine: Japan Chin and Pekingese.

BRIEF HISTORICAL SUMMARY
According to ancient documents, it is assumed that the ancestors of the Chin were presented as a gift from the rulers of Korea (during the Silla Dynasty, 377–395) to the Japanese court in 732. For a successive 100 years, there appears to have been a large number of Chins coming into Japan. Historical records also indicate that envoys sent to China (during the Tung Dynasty age 618-910) and North Korea (during the Po H'ai Dynasty age 698-926) brought back dogs of this breed directly. During the reign of the Shogunate Tsunayoshi Tokugawa (1680-1709) the breed was raised as an indoor toy dog in the Castle of Edo. In 1613 a Britisher, Captain Saris, brought a Chin to England and in 1853 Commodore Perry from the USA brought several to the US, of which two were presented to Queen Victoria of England. Since 1868, the Chin has been favoured as a lap dog by ladies of the upper classes, and currently is being widely spread as a companion dog.

GENERAL APPEARANCE
Small sized dog with broad face, covered with profuse coat, with elegant and graceful figure.

IMPORTANT PROPORTIONS
The ratio of height at withers to length of the body is equal. The body of bitches slightly longer.

BEHAVIOUR – TEMPERAMENT
Clever, mild and lovely.

HEAD (CRANIAL REGION)
SKULL
Broad and rounded.

STOP
Deep and indented.

FACIAL REGION

NOSE

Nasal bridge very short and wide, the nose on a straight line with the eyes; the nose colour black or deep flesh colour, according to the dog's markings.

TEETH

White and strong; level bite desirable, but scissors bite or undershot mouth permitted.

EYES

Large, round, set wide apart and lustrous black in color.

EARS

Long, triangular, hanging, covered with long hair; set wide apart.

NECK

Rather short, and held high.

BODY

BACK

Short and straight.

LOIN

Broad and slightly round.

CHEST

Moderately broad and deep, with ribs moderately sprung.

BELLY

Well drawn up.

TAIL

Covered with beautiful, profuse and long hair, being carried up over back.

LIMBS

FOREQUARTERS

Forearms straight, fine boned; backs of forearms below the elbow feathered.

HINDQUARTERS

Hindlegs moderately angulated, rear of the rump covered with feather.

FEET

Small and hare-shaped, covered with tufts desirable.

GAIT

Elegant, light and proud.

COAT

HAIR

Silky, straight and long. Whole body except face covered with profuse hair. The ears, neck, thighs and tail have profuse feather.

COLOR

White with markings of black or red. Markings symmetrically distributed from around eyes over whole ears as on body desirable. Especially white and wide blaze from muzzle to crown desirable.

SIZE

Height at withers: dogs approximately 25 cms, bitches slightly smaller than dogs.

FAULTS: Any departure from the foregoing points should be considered a fault and the seriousness with which the fault should be regarded should be in exact proportion to its degree. Nose: any color other than black for white with black markings; shyness; overshot mouth; solid white coat with no markings; single marking on face; wry underjaw.

N.B: Male animals should have two apparently normal testicles fully descended into the scrotum.

INTERPRETATION OF THE STANDARDS

TEMPERAMENT
The Japanese Chin is an elegant, stylish dog with a proud bearing, but a sense of fun – there is nothing cloddy or coarse about the breed. The Chin has the bearing of the aristocrat, not 'common' or undistinguished. Always happy and gay, this dog is very intelligent, but not necessarily obedient!

HEAD AND SKULL
The Standard calls for the head to be "large". This is an important feature. Small heads bring with them small squinty eyes, narrow jaws, pinched nostrils and often bad nose placements (too much length between stop and end of nose). They often lack cushion, too. For these reasons, it is important for the breed to retain a large head. The head of a Japanese Chin should be made up by a series of 'crescents'. The skull is formed by a crescent over the crown reaching from top of ear to top of ear and from top of skull to stop. Good cushioning of lips is really formed by a crescent on each side of the centre of the upper lip. These crescents form the breadth of skull required, giving the rounded appearance across the top (never domed as in a King Charles Spaniel), and also give the required rounded look in front of the skull – the forehead. "Nostrils large and black" is self-explanatory. They should be open, not pinched together, which not only spoils the look of the dog but also restricts breathing. In black and whites, "black" means black; not grey, or flesh-coloured, or 'butterfly' which is half and half. However, in red and whites the nose can be black or lighter. The muzzle is very short with little length between stop and nose. Either side of the nose must be well-cushioned, and good pigment here helps the expression. On a black and white dog, pink or unpigmented skin on the top lip just under the nose spoils the expression. These so-called 'cushions' are really fleshy parts of the muzzle above the lips on either side of the nose.

EYES
The eyes should be large, round, dark and set wide apart. They should show some white in the inner corners, which gives the required look of astonishment. They should be full of expression with a hint of laughter. A light eye spoils the expression and is hard to breed out once you get it in a line. The eye, although large and round, should not be pop or bulging which, again, gives a false expression.

EARS
A nicely-feathered or fringed ear – provided that the fringing is of good length – can set off a pretty face. If the ears are low set, this can give the impression of a domed skull. The Standard, in the colour clause, says that colour should be evenly distributed on cheeks and ears. This is interpreted to mean solid-coloured ears (not white, or with white patches or tips.)

MOUTH
Most mouths conform to the Standard by

being level or slightly undershot – this is necessary for the correct 'finish of face'. The underjaw should not 'fall away' when looked at from the outside. While it should not be prominent, it should be clearly visible when looking at the front of the head. Wry mouths are usually visible from the outside, but not always. A wry mouth is when either jaw is slightly twisted and therefore the teeth are not in alignment, but either the top or bottom jaw veers to one side. The tongue should not show. Sometimes the tip of the tongue can be seen at dead centre when the dog's mouth is closed. On closer inspection of the mouth there appears to be no logical reason for this. Some dogs only do it occasionally, and it is too bad if they are in the show ring when it happens. If the tongue protrudes to the side of the mouth, there is usually a very good reason for this, such as missing teeth or an incorrect bite. Some dogs do show their tongue as old age starts to creep up and they lose their teeth.

NECK
Proud neck carriage really means sufficient length and strength to carry the head proudly. It is this that gives that little extra elegance to a dog. If there is insufficient lay-back of shoulder, this will give a short or stuffy neck.

FOREQUARTERS
It is very important that the front legs should be absolutely straight, with no hint of crook or curve, and that the bone should be fine. If the bone is too heavy, you lose elegance and cloddiness starts to creep in. The feathering should be quite long and silky down to the feet.

BODY
The Standard is very explicit regarding a square, compactly-built dog. For this, the dog must be short in loin and the back should be level. Nothing is said in the Standard about the ribs or shape of the chest, only that the dog should be wide in chest. Well, like all dogs, the Japanese Chin has ribs. These should not be barrelled but nicely-rounded, meeting at the sternum and with good depth. By this, you will realise that the chest should not be flat. When you put your hand straight back from the front of the chest, between the front legs, if the dog is not flat-chested, the ribs meeting at the sternum should come into your hand. You should not have to raise your hand to meet a flat chest! If the dog does not present a 'square' outline but is more 'oblong', this usually means the back is too long or it is too short on the leg, which also throws out the desired square outline. The withers, of course, are the highest point of the body immediately behind the neck. This is where the upper portion of the shoulder blade and the first and second thoracic vertebrae meet.

HINDQUARTERS
Unfortunately, this is not quite as explicit as it could be but, when you think about it, if the hindquarters are straight when viewed from behind, they cannot be cow-hocked, i.e. with the hocks on each leg turning inwards to meet each other. Neither can they be bowed in hocks, the converse of cow-hocked. The Standard asks for a "good turn of stifle". The stifle joint is the knee joint, and this phraseology means that the back legs should, when viewed from the side, not be straight from hip to hock but should

狜　Chin

The illustrated Breed Standard issued by the Japanese Kennel Club.
Courtesy of The Japanese Kennel Club.

be at an angle where the upper thigh and lower thigh meet at the knee joint. This knee joint, or patella, is a particularly important part of the anatomy of all breeds, but even more so in the Toy Group. Years ago, 'slipping patellas' used to be much more prevalent in Toy Breeds than they are now. This condition occurs when the partial or complete dislocation of the knee cap takes place, slipping out of its normal placement. Often, it is very temporary and one can see it happen while a dog is moving. The patella then slips back in of its own accord. On other occasions, it is not quite so simple. When it happens, the dog usually hops, holding up the affected leg, thus moving on only three legs. Needless to say, this 'unsound' movement should be viewed very seriously by breeders and judges alike.

FEET
This really says it all – you are *not* looking for a tight, round, cat foot. The Japanese likened the foot of the Chin to the pen (brush) with which they write their alphabet.

TAIL
High set is important – it gives the right 'finish' to the square outline. If it is low set, optically it will lengthen the back. A level back is also important, not one dipping behind the shoulder or roaching. The tail must be closely curved or plumed over the back – actually the whole of the tail is plumed, i.e. the long hairs in the shape of a plume cover the entire tail. The carriage should not be straight up with a kink or a curve in the end. It is not carried sabre-fashion, but goes right over the back and the profuse feathering falls both on to the back and and down the sides of the dog.

GAIT/MOVEMENT
Straight in movement means not with the front feet converging towards each other, nor moving close together, nor crossing in front. Neither should they be wider than the chest or flicking from the pasterns – all these are faults caused by the wrong front assembly. Out at elbow, toeing out, weaving, toeing in and crabbing on the move are all faults. Lifting the feet high does not mean a hackney movement, where there is an exaggerated lift of pasterns and front feet. It is more a proud movement, giving elegance to the gait. At the rear, the legs should not move too close together and any discrepancies in construction mentioned under hindquarters will all have an adverse effect on hind movement.

COAT
When you read this clause, you can almost feel the lovely silky texture and see the beauty of a Japanese Chin in full profuse coat.

COLOUR
The first two sentences tell you exactly what is allowed. Then the Standard goes on to define the shades included in red. Sable is the one that puzzles a lot of people and some will argue it is tri-colour but, again, the Standard is very explicit. It says *never* tri-colour. It is my belief that sable is meant as a shade of red and originated as in the colour of a sable – defined in the Oxford Dictionary as a "small brown furred arctic and subarctic carnivorous quadruped allied to martens". In my time, I have actually worn (not owned) a sable coat and I can see the justification for allowing this colour as a shade of red. There is, of

course, the definition of sable as "black, as a heraldic colour" – in which case black is black, and not red tinged with black. The Kennel Club Glossary of Terms gives: "Sable Coat pattern. Black tipped hairs overlaid on a background of gold, silver, grey, fawn or tan basic coat". This brings to mind the colour clause of the Belgian Shepherd Dog Tervueren, which calls for all shades of red, fawn, grey with black overlay, though the word "sable" is not mentioned. The Standard for a sable Rough Collie is "any shade of light gold to rich mahogany or shaded sable". No mention of black here – presumably shaded sable being shaded from light gold to mahogany. My reason for going into this at length is that I have heard people refer to red and white Chins with black ear fringes and partially black leg fringes as "sable". I rest my case!

The colour clause continues with the ideal distribution of colour. Certainly mismarks do appear and this detracts from the whole picture. Flecking – small specks or particles of colour (black in black and white, and red in red and white) mixed with the white coat – probably appears more often than a real mismark (for example, half of the head solid black) and is slightly more acceptable. It is my contention that type, quality and soundness take preference over mismarks or flecking.

SIZE
Daintier – this is the critical word here, but not as in the Chihuahua Standard, which says: "...if two dogs are equally good in type the more *diminutive* preferred." The Standard does not mention "small". The two words "dainty" and "small" are not synonymous,

although it would appear they are often thought to be in the context of the Chin. To have all the things asked for in the Standard, you would have something very abnormal if you were to adhere to the premise of the smaller the better. You are not looking for – or trying to breed – a weed, nor, I might add, a giant. It is generally accepted that a larger Chin is usually more sound than a tiny one.

The word "dainty" epitomises the Japanese Chin inasmuch as it refers to "of delicate beauty" (not coarse), "scrupulously clean", which these dogs are in themselves, although not always in the house. The word also means "of delicate tastes and sensibility; fastidious; inclined to luxury". How true! I have never met one yet who did not appreciate a bit of the good life.

FAULTS
In former years UK Breed Standards included a fault clause for every breed which listed the actual faults. When the Breed Standards were rewritten in 1988, this clause was eliminated and the current phrasing, as above, is used in every Standard. The old fault clause read: "Flying ears, wry mouth, tongue showing, tri-colour". The elimination of the clause does not mean these faults no longer exist. The way in which the Standard is now written means that anything which deviates from the required definitions is a fault. The onus is now very much on the judge to decide whether any existing fault/s are sufficiently serious to withhold a prize. In other words, a judge may only withhold an award if in the opinion of the judge there is lack of sufficient merit.

COMPARISON OF THE STANDARDS

It is in the hands of breeders and judges to keep to the Standard, and not to become the slaves of fads as they come along. The art of breeding dogs is to breed to the Standard, not to change the Standard to what you are breeding.

I think the clarity of the AKC Standard is excellent. Give it to an artist who has never seen a Japanese Chin, and I believe he or she would come up with a very good likeness. It is readable and presents a clear picture to the mind.

I particularly like the substance, head and body sections. To me, the remarks about substance make it quite clear that this should be a little dog, sufficiently strong to lead a normal life, to withstand the rigours of daily life without being any way coarse, cloddy or a weed. The head clause endorses my earlier remarks, as does the body section. There are slight divergences between this Standard and some of the others. Mainly, the toeing out of the front feet; tri-colour; and height as opposed to weight.

In recent years the FCI lowered the height standard to "approximately 25 cms". This change came from the country of origin, Japan. In turn, all FCI countries were affected and it has been said that, initally, the dogs are certainly getting short on the leg and therefore out of balance in order to conform to this. Speaking personally, I do agree that some Japs are short on the leg/long in the back, but I do not feel the change in Standard has caused this, because we also see it in the UK, where the Standard remains the same.

At present, Australia and New Zealand use the British Standard. However, there is much discussion in these countries, as

Australia is now under FCI rules and will possibly be adopting its Standards. Many breeders from the Antipodes are worried because they feel that, if there is a change, they will be losing some of the important points. For example, the "characteristic look of astonishment" is not mentioned in the FCI Standard and this has always been considered an integral feature of the breed and part of its 'blueprint'. In the gait clause, no mention is made of lifting the feet high. Although the colour is given by the FCI as white with markings of black or red, no leeway is given in the red for lemon or light shades. Finally, the FCI calls for height, which is not mentioned in the KC Standard, which calls for weight instead. There is no doubt it is a bit of a 'sketchy' Standard and I, for one, would like to see it more explicit.

When the KC Breed Standard was changed it lost a lot of its 'readability', and this is what I particularly like about the American/Canadian Standards – you seem to get more of a picture when reading them than when reading either that of the KC or the FCI. In the AKC Standard, the removal of dewclaws is optional, but the practice is not mentioned in the Kennel Club Standard and dewclaws are definitely prohibited in the Japanese Standard. A major difference between the AKC Standard and those of the KC and FCI is that the front feet are permitted to point very slightly outwards, although hind feet must point straight ahead.

The coat clause is also very explicit. Colour presents a completely different picture from the KC, FCI and Japanese Standards, since the USA and Canada permit black and white with tan points.

6 *JUDGING THE JAPANESE CHIN*

Type, particularly when used in respect of a breed of dog, is an all-important word. Without understanding what it means and how it applies to the particular breed in question, it is virtually impossible to judge 'to type'. Breed type can be defined as "something serving as an illustration; similarity; likeness; uniformity; as like as two peas in a pod; typical; true to type; characteristic". Therefore, breed characteristics are all-important to determining type.

In spite of what you may hear, there is only one type – the correct type as laid down in the Japanese Chin Breed Standard. Often people say 'he is not my type', when basically they mean they do not like a dog for one reason or another. But a dog either has type, which makes it readily identifiable as a true representative of his breed, or it does not.

Many judges judge for type,

As the Japanese Chin begins to mature, the expert can assess the all-important characteristics of type, temperament and conformation.

Photo: Marc Henrie.

temperament and soundness. Type is usually the first thing we look for because, if the dog does not have breed type, it could be anything. It means the individual animal does not resemble the breed it is supposed to belong to.

If you saw a dog with a shortish, harsh coat, tail over its back, long legs, cat feet, a narrow skull, flying ears, a pointed nose, a black and white coat, and someone told you it was a Japanese Chin, you would have to say that it did not conform to breed type, even if it had a look of astonishment. So, breed type is made up by various components and one without the other is lost. As the above example shows, the general appearance of a dog, broken down into individual parts, makes up type.

In the case of the Japanese Chin all of the characteristics in the Breed Standard are essential for breed type, but these *must* be combined with the shape of the head; the characteristic look in the eyes; the ear carriage; a compact body; fine bone; straight forelegs; and the 'special' type of feet with feathering on them which are likened to the brush with which the Japanese write. Tail carriage, coat texture – these all add up to type. If one item is missing, it does not necessarily mean the dog is atypical, but if several of the important elements are missing, it surely will be.

If you aspire to judge, breed type is something you must set out to learn and thoroughly understand prior to standing in the centre of a ring to officiate. Type must come before soundness, because if a dog does not closely resemble the Standard it is not typical of the breed. Soundness must come after type – it does not matter how sound a dog is if it is not

a true representative of its breed. There are plenty of sound mongrels.

ASSESSING THE EXHIBITS

As a judge, I like to try and watch my dogs come into the ring. It can tell you quite a lot. For those few seconds they are 'natural', assuming they are walked into the ring and not carried. They are not being positioned – they should be happy, self-confident and coming in holding their own tails up! It is interesting to walk round the ring looking at the dogs and perhaps making a little noise of encouragement as you go. Most Japs respond to this and reward you with an enquiring look. Then, move them round the ring all together once or twice. This gives you an opportunity to look at them from a side view, and to check the outline, toplines, head carriage and side gait. All the time you are making mental notes, assessing what you see. In the next part of the exercise, your hands will take over and give you still more information.

ON THE TABLE

A word to the dog as you approach often puts the handler at ease! At this point, I like to assess the head properties. I do *not* make a bee-line for the mouth. I think the AKC Breed Standard gives excellent advice to a judge when it says: "if the dog displays any hesitancy, judges are asked to defer to the handler for presentation of the bite."

While looking at the head you are automatically checking the contours; the size, colour and characteristic look of the eyes; the cushion; nose placement and where the ears are placed. Then cast your eyes down and take in width of chest and position of feet (you will already have had a look at the direction in which the front feet are pointing when you make your initial walk around the ring). I check the depth of rib at this point and put my hand between the two front legs.

Moving to the side of the dog, you will move your hands over the shoulders feeling for lay-back, run your hands down the front legs to assess bone, the straightness of the legs, and where they are placed. You can feel if a dog is 'tied in front' or 'out at elbow', and you can see if he is too wide or bowed. When you move him you are able to visually confirm this. Pick up a front foot to check shape.

Topline comes next and, if you gently hold the tail up from the back with one hand and run the other down the back, you will soon feel if there is a roach and also whether the dog is short-coupled. At this point the set-on of the tail is apparent and you will have felt the texture of the coat, and observed clarity of colour, as your hand goes down the back of the dog. Both hands can then gently feel for spring of rib.

Move to the rear of the dog and gently run your hands down the quarters, without exerting any pressure. You can often feel the soundness of the patellas – or the lack of it. You have checked the rear angulation and made your assessment of the dog on the table. To complete your examination you watch the dog moving and look for style and elegance as well as soundness. Then repeat the process with the next exhibit.

YOUR FINAL ASSESSMENT
It is up to you to decide which entrant you consider is the closest to the Breed Standard and to place them accordingly. You have probably heard someone say: "if two dogs are exactly alike, you do so and so." In all my years of judging, I have never seen two dogs exactly alike. I have seen two dogs in the ring, both of which I admired tremendously and both of which, in my opinion, conformed very closely to the Breed Standard. However, in the final analysis, each excelled, in one or two different minor points, more than the other. This is where, often unwittingly, a certain amount of personal preference comes in when assessing which of the minor points you consider the most important!

THE GENTLE TOUCH AND INTEGRITY
They do not exactly go hand in hand, but both are extremely important points for the potential judge. It is of paramount importance that you, and your hands, should be as gentle with a Great Dane as with a Japanese Chin. There is never any need to be heavy-handed.

Your job as a judge is to try to bring out the best in every exhibit. Treat every exhibit and exhibitor in exactly the same way, giving each the same chance and ensure that you are polite and courteous at all times. Remember, without these 'paying customers', you would not be in the position of standing there as a judge in the first place.

You must be absolutely honest when you make your assessment. You have no friends when you stand in the middle of the ring to judge; you are there to give your honest opinion – not to bestow favours! If people who were your friends before they went into the ring are not when they come out, because they think they should have won regardless, their friendship was not worth having.

Ch. Sangria Imperial Dragon: A successful dog in the British show ring.
                                        Photo: Marc Henrie.

VARIATIONS ON A THEME

Different countries have slightly different customs. No matter where you are, when you are in the ring judging, it is *you* who are in charge of that ring.

Basically, the judging procedure is the same all over the world, but in some countries you may be asked to dictate a report on each dog. You will have a ring secretary to write down your comments.

By the way, it is an FCI rule that the ring secretary writes the report in your native language. In my experience 99.9 per cent of ring secretaries and stewards are excellent.

In most FCI countries, the steward and ring secretaries undergo special training for the job and are usually paid a nominal amount. If I know in advance I am expected to dictate a report on each exhibit, I usually take a small list of my phraseology for each breed, to help the ring secretary who may not have heard some of my expressions. In FCI countries there are usually at least two people in the ring – one to write and one to call the dogs into the ring, check their numbers and line them up before you start judging. Depending on the country and the amount of paperwork involved there is sometimes an extra person helping out.

Even if it is your first time judging overseas – and we all have to start with a first time – you will have been sent a book of Guidelines for Judges. All the Scandinavian countries are particularly good at this, and their booklets are well-written and easy to understand. At their larger shows they have a judges' briefing. You will have read and memorised as much as you can and, as far as the judging is concerned, you will please yourself. The paperwork is slightly different, but your ring stewards will be very helpful here.

American ring procedure is easy if you remember the one major difference to judging in other countries – it is your responsibility to check the dogs into the ring and to check for absentees. The steward does not do this for you. The judge also gives out the ribbons, not the ring steward. In my experience, ring stewards in America know their job well and never try to interfere with – or influence – the judge.

Judging in the UK must be something of a nightmare for overseas judges. At Championship Shows there are usually more dogs in a class than most other countries. Classification is quite different, featuring Tyro, Post Graduate and Mid Limit, to name but a few. The best advice I can give is to study your schedule –

which will be sent to you before the show, and will list the number of dogs in each class. The schedule gives the definition of each class, which usually depends on age or previous awards. In the UK, the same dog is often entered in more than one class. This is marked in a different way in the judging book, and the steward usually places the 'seen' dogs at the end of the 'new' dogs in each class. It is normal to place five dogs, and they must be placed in order from one to five, not in reverse order. The UK Kennel Club issues a Guideline for Judges which should be sent to every judge prior to his or her appointment to award CCs in a breed for the first time. It is also sent to all overseas judges when they are first approved to award CCs in Britain. The show secretary, not the Kennel Club, sends these out.

JUDGING TIPS

There is nothing worse than a ring steward who follows you round, standing at your shoulder, and possibly making remarks while you are judging. Remember, this is your ring and you are the person doing the judging. Just politely ask them to go and sit down.

Give some thought to what you are going to wear before you go to the show. It does not really apply to Japanese Chins, but there is nothing worse than a judge in a smart suit or dress judging one of the larger breeds and becoming visibly annoyed when a dog slobbers on them slightly or jumps up. Be comfortable, be smart, and consider the size of dogs you are judging, so that you avoid sleeves or jewellery dangling in the face of table dogs as you go over them. Make sure your shoes are comfortable and easy to walk and stand in. It must be miserable to have your feet complaining while you are trying to concentrate on judging.

Whenever or wherever you are judging, do get to the venue at least 30 minutes before judging is due to commence. Make yourself known to the secretary, and find out where your ring is located. If you are judging in Britain there is very little preliminary work to do before you commence judging – just explain to your steward where you want your dogs lined up. You do not have to do this in other countries, but you will probably have a lot of papers to sign before you start judging.

It is therefore advisable to get to your ring at least half an hour before judging is due to begin.

Of course you will be nervous on your first judging engagement but, once you see the dogs and start to think about them, your fears should soon disappear if you know your job and have done your homework. I still get butterflies at every show but, as soon as the first dog comes into the ring, I have a lot to think about and become so absorbed that the butterflies are gone.

7 CELEBRATION OF THE JAPANESE CHIN

The breed has featured in many beautiful works of art. The magnificent book *Dog Painting 1840-1940* by William Secord (The Antique Collectors' Club 1992) has several examples of the work of the artist Frances Fairman (English, 1836-1923) depicting our breed. Miss Fairman was a member of the Ladies Kennel Association, and was herself a breeder and exhibitor of Japanese Chins. Her paintings of Queen Alexandra's Japanese Chins and also Lady Samuelson's stock are superb examples of her work.

Maud Earl (English, 1864-1943) is among the best-known artists who regularly depicted the Japanese Chin in her paintings. She was a prolific artist who was commissioned by royalty, and a very good example of her work featuring the Japanese Chin can be found in the series of photogravures reproduced by the

A painting of two Japanese Chins by the 20th century artist Annie Shenton.

Photo courtesy: Sara Davenport.

A painting in oil on silk by Eva Swindell, featuring Peggy Lanceley's Ch. Barabelle Blueanton.

Photo: David Evans.

Berlin Photographic Company (No. 17, 1903). Before she emigrated to New York, Miss Earl executed a painting entitled *The Allies*. Five breeds appeared: the Japanese Spaniel; the Belgian Griffon; the Russian Borzoi; the French Bulldog; and the British Bulldog. The work was commissioned by *The Illustrated London News* and appeared as a supplement in its edition of June 12th 1915.

Lilian Cheviot was a wonderful artist, and her paintings of Pekingese are well-known and much admired. David Roche of Australia was kind enough to send us a

copy of the portrait of Mrs Samuel Smith's Oriental Kusadama. Kusadama (weight five lbs.) won a Challenge Certificate at Richmond Show in 1914 under Miss Dagois. He was born on January 22nd 1913, and was sired by Oriental Toshimo out of the great brood, Noma.

The English miniaturist and painter of animal portraits, Annie Shenton, was known to have exhibited at the Royal Academy twice in 1904. Little is known about her except that she lived in West Kensington, London, and included the Japanese Chin in her works.

Other artists known to have painted the Japanese Chin include Gertrude Saville, another breeder and exhibitor – examples of her work can still be found today. Miss Beatrice Clennel painted a lovely portrait of Ch. Mr Weejum and Charming Billy. The well-known Northern artist, Eva Swindell, painted a head study of Peggy Lanceley's Ch. Barabelle Blueanton in oil on silk. Miss Swindell has captured the dog's expression perfectly.

The German Empress, Augusta, owned two Japanese Chins – Itti, a bitch, and Fumi, a dog. The noted animal artist Heinrich Sperling (1844-1924) worked mainly from Berlin. He painted them together and also captured Itti on canvas by herself. The painting of Itti is now is Sweden – probably the oldest picture of a Chin in that country, as there were no Chins in Sweden at the time the painting was executed. Sadly, Itti died in whelp and it was reported that Fumi died shortly afterwards "of a broken heart".

THE CHIN IN PRINT
The book *My Mother Told Me* by Charles Chenevix Trench tells the true story of

The Japanese Spaniel and the Rising Sun.

The Japanese Spaniel

Saki and his adventures with the author's family and Turk, a brindle Bull Terrier, in the Far East. The book is great fun and guaranteed to appeal to any lover of the Japanese Chin.

The breed has featured in two works of fiction, as far as we can ascertain. *Big Brother Bob*, written in 1923 by R. Scotland Liddell, is illustrated with photographs taken by the author. Bob is a shaggy mongrel with a hint of Bearded Collie about him, and his little brother is Prince Ito – a red and white Japanese Chin with an aristocratic manner and a retroussé nose. The author was obviously a lover of our breed, as he writes with great accuracy about the Japanese Chin's foibles and habits. The story is sad in parts, because Ito feels deserted when his master leaves him to go overseas during the Great War. Eventually all turns out well and the story ends with the two old dogs living out their lives together.

The children's book *Our Paying Guests* by 'Tiny' is quite amusing. Tiny is a smooth fox terrier and gives us her account of her 'Mammy's' adventures looking after a variety of dogs and cats. Among the guests are a litter of Japanese Chin puppies, and the tale does not have a happy ending! The book is amply illustrated with Thomas Fall photographs, including Queen Alexandra with her Japanese Chins and Lady Samuelson with five of her dogs.

The breed is featured on scores of postcards and to a lesser degree on stamps and cigarette cards. Some good photographs of early dogs can be found on cigarette cards, and named dogs include Mrs Bartleet's Ch. Yoshiteru of Mikazuki, Mrs Mosscockle's Ch. General Kuroki of Braywick and Mrs Lloyd's Ch. Royal Yama Hito.

Many music-hall stars and actresses were pictured holding the breed in publicity postcards and these are most collectable. Art Deco cards featuring

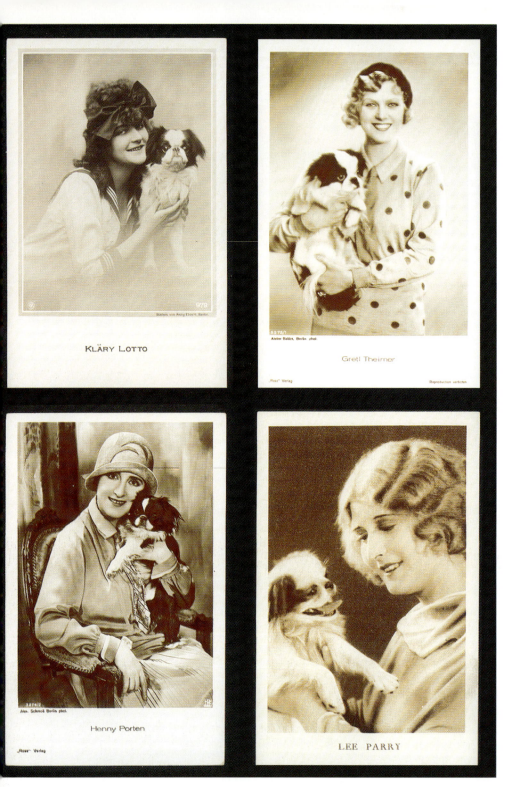

KLÄRY LOTTO

Gretl Theimer

Henny Porten

LEE PARRY

*The breed is featured on many postcards, and these are
always highly sought-after.   Photo courtesy: Paul Keevil.*

glamorous women with their Japanese Chins can be found, many executed by the Italian artist Bertigula. The stamp and postcard expert Paul Keevil rates his favourite postcard as being from the Frowde Hodder and Stoughton series which depicts dogs' heads in front of their national flags. Apparently, the Japanese Chin with the Rising Sun is one of the hardest to locate in this series!

CHINS ON FILM AND TV

The breed has featured in several films. *Four Frightened People,* made by Paramount in 1934, was based on the novel by E. Arnot Robertson and was directed by Cecil B. de Mille. It starred Claudette Colbert and Herbert Marshall. The story features a group of people who escape from a plague-infested ship and flee through the Malaysian jungle to find civilisation. Miss Colbert fights her way through the jungle with her Japanese

Chin tucked under her arm. The dog is of a good type and, although he is not seen moving, he is reported as having taken all the filming in his stride. The movie did not win critical acclaim. *Variety* said: "The adventures are episodic and disjointed, running the gamut from stark tragedy to unbelievable." *Literary Digest* described it as "a cumbersome sort of melodrama...despite some mildly entertaining jungle scenes".

The British Technicolour film of 1950, *The Elusive Pimpernel,* boasted a strong cast: David Niven, Margaret Leighton, Cyril Cusack and Ch. Kin-Sen of Yevot! The film was not well received. Richard Mallett, writing in *Punch,* stated: "I never thought that I should feel inclined to leave a Powell and Pressburger film before the end, but I did." Some of the film was shot on location in Bath, and Kin-Sen was recruited to play the part of Henrietta – the constant companion of Lord Anthony

Ch. Kin-Sen, star of 'The Elusive Pimpernel', investigates her stuffed toy stand-in, with Miss Tovey (pictured right) and Mrs Saddler.

Dewhurst (David Hutcheson). In one scene, Henrietta has to run, by herself, down a flight of highly polished marble stairs at Lord Granville's Ball. This remarkable scene was accomplished by means of Miss Tovey crouching at the foot of the stairs – out of camera range – giving welcoming hand signals to Henrietta. She stepped out like a veteran giving the impression that she spent her days on nothing less than gleaming marble!

The film certainly brought Kin-Sen fame, if not fortune. The *Sunday Pictorial* and *Sunday Graphic* newspapers both featured her. The *Graphic* reported: "Most beginners (in the film industry) have to be content with a walk-on part – Kinney gets carried everywhere!" She was recognised by travellers at Paddington station, and even made a guest appearance to raise funds for the Conservative Party. Her fee for the scenes filmed in Bath was 50 guineas. This was donated to the Methodist Missionary Society Hospital in Chaotung, SW China which was run by Miss Tovey's nephew, Dr Frank Tovey FRCS. The film's director and producer were so taken with Kin-Sen that they arranged for her to attend the London studios for some more scenes with Margaret Leighton and David Hutcheson. The fee for these appearances was donated to Mrs Winnie Barber's appeal for the Animal Health Trust.

More recently, Vera and Leland Schenck, well-known Japanese Chin breeders in California, provided dogs for several movies including *The King's Thief* and others about court life. They also were in demand for television appearances.

The famous British breeder, Miss Tovey, was always eager to publicise the breed. An invitation to appear on the renowned BBC TV children's magazine programme, *Blue Peter*, was received in 1966. The programme always featured animals in general and dogs in particular and, to this day, it is customary for the Crufts BIS winner to make a studio appearance on the show. The Yevot animals went to Lime Grove studios for the show, which was broadcast live.

A dog and bitch, together with four puppies, were required for the programme. Sadly, however, the strain of the day was too much for two of the puppies and they died the next day. The puppies had been destined to go to Mrs Kangassalo in Finland, and two others were sent in their place. The show certainly provided good coverage of the breed, and their appearance generated enquiries from UK viewers who were interested in purchasing a puppy. Some years later, Miss Tovey again appeared on television with the Yevots, in a programme featuring the well-known broadcaster, Johnny Morris. The Yevots were shown in their home surroundings being prepared for a day out at Bath Championship Show, and this too provided good publicity for the breed.

TALES, LEGENDS AND FABLES
The breed has several legends or fables woven around it. During the research for this book, many delightful tales came to light. We hope they will interest you, as they did us, and so we are happy to share them with you.

From a book written in 1880 entitled *Indian Notes about Dogs*, under the heading *Japanese and Chinese Dogs*, we came across the following snippets:

*A delightful pen
and ink sketch by
Lillian Tiffany.*

"The writer, having travelled in Japan and also having served in the China War of 1860, when the sacking of the Emperor's Summer Palace caused the Chinese Pugs found therein to become fashionable pets in Europe, can find nothing to say in favour of either Japanese or Chinese dogs as they are utterly useless for sport or killing vermin.

"Doubtless the fashionable taste for these dogs will, like other fashions, die out as they are not to be compared to the genuine Maltese for ladies' pets.

"When the writer was in Japan, the great test of excellence was for the purchaser to endeavour to rest a silver dollar (about double the size of a rupee) on its rim on the animal's nose. If he could do so, the price was half what it would otherwise be, as the prominent eye and extremely short nose of the perfect specimen rendered the attempt impossible."

Here is Sir Edwin Arnold's description in verse of the Japanese Chin from *About Our Dogs* by A. Croxton Smith.

Our doggies came dancing this morning and said,
With a touch of their paw, and a glance of their head:
"Play with me."
Each Japanese Chin came kissing

A Japanese postcard.

The breed has many devoted owners and admirers – none more so than Lynn Seymour, the great ballerina and actress, who is pictured with Yeosinga Jade Mermaid.

Photo: Marc Henrie.

my hand
    And trying to make me understand:
    "Play with me."
    I played with them all: now wouldn't you play
    When sweet little angels dance up and say:
    "Play with me."

Another of our favourites was originally reproduced in a Japanese Chin Club Bulletin in 1967. It was brought to our attention again by Mrs Ann Dilley.

The origin of the Japanese Lion Dog
"Once upon a time a very holy follower of Buddha retired into the jungles of Korea for prayer and meditation. This saintly person seems to have fared better than St Francis of Assisi, for he learnt the language of the jungle creatures before he preached to them. All the beasts would come to him for advice and consolation in their troubles, and among others, the lion laid his matrimonial difficulties before the hermit.

"The lion was in great distress as he had fallen deeply in love with the marmoset, and the lady, though possibly flattered, had pointed out that their union was impossible owing to their difference in size. Perhaps, she added, she would always be a sister to him, but the lion was not to be consoled with such a promise.

"The Holy Man considered the problem and then addressed the lion as follows: 'If your love for this lesser one is so great, you should make some sacrifice to obtain her'.

'That will I gladly do,' said the King of the Beasts.

'Will you sacrifice your great strength

Miss Peggy Guggenheim – the great American art collector with one of her Japanese Chins.

and become the least among the beasts to win her?' was the reply.

'Even that will I do,' said the lion.

'Then your wish shall be granted,' said the hermit and recited a prayer, by virtue of which the lion dwindled until he had assumed the dimensions of the marmoset.

'Are you still of the same mind?' enquired the hermit, 'now that you know how it feels to be small and feeble?'

'Yes, I am content, if only she will love me,' was the reply.

'This is love indeed,' said the Saint, 'Your steadfastness shall be rewarded. Though you have lost your great strength, you shall retain your courage and your royal dignity; hunger shall no longer force you to go hunting, for the meat for your offspring shall be provided at the tables of the great and you will bear the insignia of royalty. Also to you shall be added the joyous spirit of the little monkeys who know neither care nor labour, but live contentedly, beneath the sun.'

"So the lovers were married and lived happily ever after, and the offspring of their union was the Imperial Japanese."

8 BREEDING JAPANESE CHIN

You have decided you would like a litter of puppies. Hopefully, this is because you have shown your Japanese Chin bitch, she has done well and you are 'hooked' on the showing scene and want to try to breed something a little better than you have already got. You may be considering breeding for any of the following reasons:
a) Your vet said it would be good for the bitch to have a litter
b) You think she is sweet and would like another just like her
c) You want to make money.

If any of the above is the case, then my advice is: "Forget it!" Perhaps this is a good time to say that Japanese Chins are not a commercial breed and I, for one, hope they never become one. Generally speaking, you will get one to five puppies in a litter. Out of these you will be extremely fortunate if you have a potential champion.

THE STUD DOG
No matter how good your bitch is, the qualities of the stud dog are inevitably going to play a major part in the resultant progeny of such a union. It takes two to make a bargain, to tango and also to produce the best possible puppies.

Ch. Sternroc Kabuki, Ch. Sternroc Biki, Ch. Sternroc Cho Cho of Gorsedene and Ch. Sternroc Kiki. The aim of every breeder is to produce a line of dogs that are sound in body and mind, and share breed type.

Photo: Thomas Fall.

Ch. Sternroc Ju-Jitsu: An important stud dog for the Sternroc kennel.

Photo: Thomas Fall.

Be honest with yourself and assess your bitch's good and bad points. You are looking for a stud dog whose attributes are at least as good as those of your bitch and, hopefully, better. If your bitch has light eyes and you breed to a stud dog whose eyes are also light, the possibility of getting a litter of dark-eyed puppies are less than they would be had you chosen a dark-eyed sire. If your bitch has a bad front, and the sire you are thinking of has a good front but is cow-hocked, think again. The closer you breed, the more you will be doubling up on both good and bad points. I have successfully bred father to daughter in several breeds. I am not saying both were perfect specimens, but I am saying neither had glaring faults.

Do not pick a stud dog just because he is the latest Champion or someone else got a nice litter from him – his pedigree might not tie up with that of your bitch. Also, if the dog is what you want, be prepared to travel. Do not go to the stud dog down the road just because it is

handy. There is no hard and fast way to produce a Champion. Think of all the geneticists who breed dogs. Do they produce even one Champion in every litter?

I do not happen to believe that you should have brood bitches at home and another string of show bitches. Mine have always been multi-purpose. Clever breeders, in all breeds, can and do produce litter after litter, from different bitches or stud dogs, of excellent breed type and with several strong breed points in which they excel. This is breeding to type, and it is the reason why people can say from which kennel dogs come because they look so alike. In breeding, there is a certain amount of chance, quite a lot of good animal husbandry, and the knowledge that you cannot make a silk purse out of a sow's ear.

THE MATING
Before deciding to mate your Japanese Chin bitch, make absolutely certain that

you will be free to look after her about the time she is due to whelp and afterwards until the puppies are fully weaned. If you have commitments which prevent this, then your bitch should not be mated.

You have made your choice of stud dog. Your bitch is in excellent physical condition, she has been wormed and vaccinated and you are now waiting for her to come into season. You will already have contacted the owner of the stud dog, seen a copy of the potential sire's pedigree and, hopefully, actually seen the dog for yourself. You will have ascertained the stud fee, and told the owner of the stud dog approximately when you expect your bitch to come in season.

The great day arrives and she starts to show colour. A few bitches have colourless seasons but, in my experience with Japanese Chins, this is relatively rare. Phone the stud dog owner to say that you expect her to be ready to mate in about ten days time and that you will keep in touch. Then make arrangements for the place and time of mating. When the discharge goes from red to straw colour, and the vulva is still swollen, this is normally the time the bitch will be receptive to the dog. If you gently wiggle your finger on one side of the outside of the vulva she will often hold her tail to one side. This is another indication of her readiness.

I have always mated Japanese Chins inside the house or office, and let the dog and bitch play together for a few moments first. When the dog starts to mount the bitch, put her on a table covered with a towel and pick up the dog and put him on the table at her rear. It is usually a matter of a few seconds before

he mounts and penetrates her. Some dogs 'tie' for just a few minutes, others for as long as fifteen or twenty minutes, but let them 'break' naturally. Some dogs penetrate but do not tie, and this can still be a successful mating.

PRE-WHELPING CARE
Now you have nine weeks (sixty three days) to wait for the results! Your bitch will continue to lead a normal, active life. Do let her have regular exercise but, as the whelping date draws closer, you will often find that she will prefer to take her daily stroll a little more gently, so shorten the distance. Do not let her climb or jump once she has been mated.

Personally, if a bitch of mine were entered for a dog show after she had been mated, I would not take her. My reason is that the health and well-being of the bitch and her prospective litter are paramount. She may be perfectly all right going to a show but, on the other hand, she could pick up kennel cough, fall off the table when being examined, or even get accidentally bitten or frightened by another dog. Your decision is all a matter of personal preference, but I do not believe in taking chances in these circumstances.

I firmly believe that when you are thinking about rearing puppies, you must start well before the puppies are born, even, in fact, before they are conceived. It is no use mating a weedy, wormy bitch and hoping for lovely fat, healthy puppies. Far better to start with a properly reared bitch, in the pink of condition, and go on from there.

FEEDING
All of our grown dogs are fed twice a day,

and we do not increase the feed of a bitch in whelp until the beginning of the fifth week. Again, all of our dogs get fresh milk and egg yolks as part of their usual diet. At the onset of the fifth week, we usually increase the amount of meat for the expectant mother and, for the last two or three weeks, feed an extra little meal mid-day. We also step up the amount of milk available. I have always fed all of the Japs two meals a day, except young puppies and pregnant bitches who get more, and I have never used an all-in-one meal. I use meat, chicken, fish and soaked wholewheat biscuit meal. The meat can be raw tripe, raw mince, and sometimes cooked chicken or cooked and well-boned fish.

Each dog is different and, as Japs are not really greedy, you will be able to work out, by trial and error, exactly how much to feed your pregnant bitch. Better, in this case, to err on the side of too much than too little.

CONTACTING YOUR VET
Giving birth is a natural process and should be achieved with no complications whatsoever. If this is the first litter for you and your bitch, my first piece of advice is not to panic. Secondly, it might be wise to tell your veterinary surgeon the date on which your bitch is due to whelp, in case you need help and because you will need to know he or she is readily available. Ring again about a week before your bitch's due date to let the practice know how she is getting on and to check the vet will be somewhere handy, should an emergency arise.

It seems to be the vogue nowadays to have a bitch scanned during her pregnancy to see how many puppies she is carrying. I have never had this done. Of course, I have been fortunate in that my partner is a veterinary surgeon – one of the old school who can accurately palpate a bitch at three weeks and usually let you know, not only that she is in whelp, but how many puppies to expect.

THE DELIVERY
You will have given some thought to where your puppies will be born and will have a whelping box in readiness. My Japanese Chins have always whelped in my bedroom. I use a wooden box on feet, with a lid that opens and a wire front on a wooden frame, which also opens.

I make sure the whelping boxes are meticulously scrubbed well before the time for them to be used, and always give them a final wash-out with a disinfectant solution. Then I line the box with clean newspaper and put a small cardboard box (about half the size of the whelping box itself) inside the whelping box. Into the cardboard box (which is actually a small supermarket carton with a section cut out to give the bitch easy access) I put a layer of newspaper and a snug rug.

Three weeks before the bitch is due to whelp I put her into this box in the location where I intend the whelping to take place. In this way the bitch gets used to her surroundings, and there is nothing to worry her when the time comes. For ten days before my bitches are due to whelp, I make sure they are checked every three to four hours day and night. Both bitch and puppies are very precious, and I believe no trouble should be spared.

When the bitch shows signs of whelping (scratching and/or straining), remove the snug rug from the inner box and add more newspaper. Make sure that someone is sitting with the bitch from the time she starts to prepare herself to give birth, even if it is in the middle of the night. I am a great believer in sitting and watching and, if she is able to cope without help, it is better for her to do so. I never cease to marvel how wonderful nature is and how a bitch knows just what to do, even with her first litter of puppies.

THE WHELPING

Do have an 'emergency kit' handy in case you have to help. This should consist of three or four old, clean towels which can be used to rub the puppies dry; some white cotton to be used if the bitch is unable to bite the umbilical cord (the cotton is tied round the cord about half an inch from the puppy's body and the cord is torn from the far side, which is attached to the afterbirth); a hot-water bottle, filled with hot but not boiling water, wrapped in a towel and placed in another lined cardboard box nearby (this will be used to put the puppy on while the bitch is producing another, or while you are cleaning her up); household scales on which to weigh each puppy.

After each puppy is born and the bitch is busy licking the puppy, and after she has severed the umbilical cord, take away the afterbirth each time while she is expelling another whelp. Roll each afterbirth in newspaper and dispose of it. Then add more clean newspaper to the box. This saves disturbing the bitch to take up soiled papers each time she has a whelp. If the puppies come very quickly and she does not have time to look after the one previously born while giving birth to another, rub the first one dry, very gently, in a towel. This is done in front of the bitch so that she can see it happening,

then the puppy is either put to her or placed temporarily in the box with the hot-water bottle until she is ready to have it with her.

When your bitch has finished whelping, put the puppies into the box with the hot-water bottle until the whelping box is quickly cleaned out, then mother and babies should be snugly settled into the hot-water bottle box placed within the whelping box. This way, the new mother is allowed room to move around in the area between the cardboard box and the whelping box itself. However, she should be taken out at regular intervals to relieve herself. She will not want to stay away from her babies for long, so stay with her, watch her, and, as soon as she is ready, bring her back indoors.

When whelping is over, the bitch will probably appreciate a drink of glucose and water, or warm milk and honey or glucose.

No two whelpings are the same, and this is purely basic whelping procedure. If you have any problems or suspect complications, telephone your veterinary surgeon immediately, regardless of time, and be guided by the advice you receive.

POST-WHELPING

Often a bitch does not want to eat much for the first few hours, or even a day, after she has had her puppies. Offer her some light food such as scrambled or coddled eggs or a little boiled fish. She will need plenty of small, tempting meals for the first few days, and will appreciate the extra cosseting.

Most Japs are very good mothers and it really is an effort to get them to leave their babies for the first few weeks, even to relieve themselves. They dash right

Once weaning is under way, the puppies become increasingly independent.

Photo: Marc Henrie.

back into the whelping box as soon as they can. Keep a regular check on the puppies to make sure they all get their fair share at the 'milk bar', and if one is not suckling, try to hold that puppy on to the teat. If this does not work, consult your vet.

Try not to disturb the puppies any more than possible. If they are warm, dry and not crying, do not pick them up, as this can upset the dam. Make sure the bitch has a drink of milk, or milk and water, available at all times while she is nursing puppies. A word of warning – do put the bowl where an adventurous puppy (or even one that has had the temerity to hold on hard to the teat and perhaps come out of the whelping box still hanging on) cannot fall into it.

CARE OF THE PUPPIES
On the second or third day after the puppies are born they should have their dewclaws removed. It is not necessary for a veterinary surgeon to do this, provided you know someone who is experienced and competent enough to do this for you.

A stud dog owner who is an experienced breeder may well do this for you but, if not, call your vet.

Do not let strangers (or anybody else for that matter) come and look at the puppies or for quite some time. I once had a bitch with very young puppies in a room with the door closed and specifically asked a member of the family not to go past the door (dogs do recognise footsteps, you know). This person disregarded the request and the bitch was sufficiently upset to kill one of her puppies. Breeders, the owner of the sire or potential purchasers may want to see the puppies as soon as possible, but remember they can bring in disease and upset the dam. Let them all wait until the puppies are fully-weaned and romping around. That is the best time for a prospective purchaser, or any other breeders who may be interested, to look at the puppies.

WEANING
We start our puppy weaning with a mixture of Farex (baby food) and glucose

mixed with warm milk, gradually introducing meat. If you have a blender, you will find that puppies adore such things as a little chicken cooked with onion and carrot and blended to a puree – they greedily lap this up very quickly. From there, we usually introduce fine minced meat, scalded with a nice gravy, and I am a firm believer in wholewheat biscuit meal.

We give our puppies five meals a day – three milk and two meat – gradually decreasing the meals. By the time they are six months they are on a milky breakfast, followed by a meat meal and another meal later in the day, and they are offered a drink of milk last thing at night. We used to keep goats, because we believe that goats' milk is the finest thing for rearing puppies, and they certainly seemed to thrive on it.

Never let your puppies go to their new homes until they are fully vaccinated, or have at least had their first vaccination in a course of two. Warn the new owner not to take the puppy out of their own home and garden until ten days after the second vaccination. It adds a bit to the purchase price, but when your Japanese Chin puppy leaves you, you will know that you have done your best for the puppy and given it a good start for life in its new home.

Do not forget to make up some feeding charts, and it is also advisable to give small quantities of the food you are using to the new owners so that the puppy will not suffer any discomfort through sudden changes of diet. This is only the beginning – you should also be prepared to offer an 'after sales service' to any purchaser and be prepared to take your puppy back if it does not settle in its new home. Be a responsible breeder – do not rely on dog rescue organisations.

9 MODERN BRITISH BREEDERS

The 1950s were an exciting time for the Japanese Chin. Several new faces rose to prominence in the breed, although Yevot and Riu Gu were dominant. Nesta Alexander (Sandycuft) was highly successful with the red and white, Ch. Yen Suki of Yevot, who gained his title in 1951. His first CC came from Miss Tovey (a win that would be regarded as controversial today!), but he quickly gained his title under Mrs Barber and Mr Corbett, and then went on to win a further five CCs. A repeat mating of this dog in 1952 produced Miss Tovey's great sire and winner, Ch. Shira Tama of Yevot.

The adult bitch, Mitsu of Riu Gu, noted for her exquisite hare feet and well-cushioned muzzle, then joined the Sandycuft kennel and she gained her title in 1953. The early 1960s saw Mrs Alexander hit the high spots with two more bitches bred by Mrs Craufurd, Ch. Sandycuft Etoile of Riu Gu and Ch. Sandycuft Maiko of Riu Gu.

Miss M. Fulleylove campaigned Ch. Julietta of Riu Gu to her title and, with her sister, she bred some top-quality stock under the Honshu affix. Miss Tovey's Sostenuto of Honshu gained her title in

1961. Later in the 1960s, Toshita of Honshu gave a good account of himself when mated to Niju Kokuseki No Riu Gu – a daughter of the imported Japanese bitch – by siring the lovely Ch. O'Kayama of Riu Gu for Mrs Craufurd. Owing to illness, the Misses Fulleylove had been unable to show Toshita and so he went to Mrs Craufurd, who wrote: "It would be hard to find a more charming dog, he strode through the tough pack here who accepted him as one of themselves, only Ch. Pierre of Kurraba had previously been accorded the same happy reception."

A MODEL OF THE BREED
Pierre was born on September 27th 1954. By Ch. Perseus of Riu Gu ex Susan of Kurraba (a daughter of Ch. Tangerine of

Ch. Pierre of Kurraba.

Maywood ex Fleur of Abbey Cottage), he won his first CC in 1955 under the late Mr W. McDonald Daly. He went on to win 18 CCs, a breed record that stood for many years. Little used at stud, his litter sister Marielou was mated to Maxi of Maywood to produce the influential Ch. Mitzi of Maywood.

Bryan Mitchell, writing in *Our Dogs* in 1984, had this to say about Pierre: "Not a small dog, Pierre's head was a model, round in all details, a series of circles and crescents. He was the right shape and had coat in abundance. He had style, magnificence, presence, a magic all his own. Those who knew him still think of him as an unequalled model for the breed."

NAVY VILLAS

No one in the UK has been actively involved in the breed longer than Margaret Journeaux. A former president of the Japanese Chin Club (currently a vice-president) and a Crufts judge, Margaret has devoted her life to the breed, and it is a passion she shares with her family.

As a child, Margaret was a Jersey resident when the German Army occupied the Channel Islands at the start of the war. Margaret was given a black and white Chin as a gift by his owners, who were fleeing the occupied islands. His name was Oki and he went everywhere with Margaret, riding in the basket attached to the handlebars of her bicycle. They formed a mutual admiration society, and Oki was adored by his lucky new owner.

Oki had been bred by the Mitchells who were the first people to have Japanese Chins in Jersey. He was one of a

Margaret Journeaux with Navy Villas Tuzika: Winner of the Toy Group at the Jersey Summer Show 1981 under Ellis Hulme.

litter of nine sired by a Swiss dog out of an English dam, all of whom survived. Mrs Mitchell was a wealthy woman, who had been an actress in her youth. The dogs had every possible luxury. Margaret struck up a friendship with Mrs Mitchell which lasted until the latter's death at the age of 90. Years later, Margaret was to give Mrs Mitchell several Navy Villas Chins and these gave her friend great pleasure.

Margaret and Bevan were married at Christmas in 1944 and, in 1946, Bevan suggested they should buy a wife for Oki. Through an address obtained in the canine press, they wrote to Constance Jameson of the world-famous Redcedars Kennels. Eventually, a black and white bitch puppy arrived in Jersey. Oki adored his new-found friend but, at the age of seven, sex held no attractions for him and the friendship failed to develop into a mating, much to the Journeaux' disappointment. Soon, however, two red and white dogs, sired by Miss Jameson's Champions, arrived in Jersey, and Margaret and Bevan Journeaux joined the Jersey Dog Club. Success in the show ring was immediate and breeding was undertaken, with some of the puppies finding their way back to England.

Navy Villas dogs were in demand around the world. Peter Pan and Petti Sing gained their titles in Canada, and Madame Raquet from France imported Navy Villas Yoki and Navy Villas Kathe, who both gained their titles. Mrs Bylord in Holland had a pair of Navy Villas as much-loved pets, and another brace went to Paris.

Navy Villas' involvement in the show scene led to an invitation, in the early 1950s, to stay with Mrs Craufurd who was hosting a 'doggy' garden party. Margaret took along the red and white Kyo of Redcedars. She was pleased to win a third prize with him, as he was in competition with all the great names of the Chin world. The trip from Jersey was in a tiny plane to Stansted airport, and Margaret remembers that Peggy Searl was working for Mrs Craufurd at the time. A warm friendship developed between Mrs Craufurd and the young Margaret and future visits to England nearly always meant a trip to Glebe House to see Mrs

Craufurd and her 60 or so Japanese Chins.

As the 1950s drew to a close Margaret and Bevan decided that it was time for dog shows and breeding to take a back seat, and their eldest daughter, Jill, was born in 1959. They had twin daughters, Sue and Fiona, five years later and Margaret tells us "with three children and ten Japanese Chins we were kept very busy!"

A Riu Gu bitch joined Navy Villas, and Mrs Craufurd took Navy Villas stock back to England to incorporate into Riu Gu lines and to show. Francine Macey was a resident of Jersey who had approached Margaret to buy a puppy. Unfortunately, Margaret had nothing to sell her at the time and Francine purchased a dog and bitch puppy from Mrs May Robertshaw, who had a very well-established Pekingese kennel and was breeding some attractive Japanese Chins. The two puppies were mostly Yevot breeding and eventually Margaret bought three puppies from Francine.

One of these, Franling Sand Piper, was sent over to Miss Sully to be mated and taken to Mrs Craufurd's Ch. Yama Kiko of Riu Gu. This mating resulted in the dog, Navy Villas Sokai. When mated to Margaret's Franling Notiko, he produced Navy Villas Osho. Osho was probably Margaret's biggest winner in the UK, as he won two CCs in very stiff competition. Had his owner not faced such a difficult and expensive journey to the mainland, he would undoubtedly have gained his title.

Over the last few years, Margaret has not been able to show the Navy Villas as often as she would have wished, but the line continues and is especially noted for its beautiful deep red and whites. They lead free and natural lives, and are very much cherished by their devoted owners.

AN EXPORT BOOM

The breed was in demand abroad, and British breeders were sending stock around the world. The Oudenarde Kennel was well-known and successful with a variety of breeds and, when Mesdames Hamilton and Temple decided to breed Japanese Chins, they based their line on a bitch from Miss Miles, Ma Lou of Maywood. Ma Lou was mated to Ch. Pegasus of Riu Gu to produce Ch. Oudenarde Pikko.

Working closely with Sheila Tarry (Penwarne), they went on to produce other good winners, including Oudenarde Spritely who won one CC. Spritely was mated to Ch. Mosaru of Yevot, resulting in Oudenarde Sugar Puff – as we have seen, the first UK dog to be exported to Japan.

Miss Kathleen Sully had started her Camplane kennel in the early 1950s with a bitch, Nishida of Yevot, purchased from Miss Tovey. Nishida proved to be a good foundation for the kennel, producing Princess Yone. Nishida lived to the age of 11, and was behind many winners. Princess Kuchi Nashi gained her title in 1962, while her brother, Prince Shogun of Camplane, was mated to Cha Rose to produce Prince Shogun of Kurraba Tu. Prince Shogun of Camplane was sold to Holland, and other exports made their mark around the world.

Int. and Nor. Ch. Camplane Kappa became an influential sire in Scandinavia. A great devotee of the red and white, Miss Sully's second Champion was a bitch in this colour, Ione of Camplane. She gained her title in 1968, the same year

that Mrs Sharp campaigned the group-winning Prince Mikasa of Camplane to his title. Plans to mate Princess Kirin of Camplane to the great Nyorai came unstuck, due to an outbreak of foot and mouth disease and a subsequent restriction on the movement of livestock. However, a later trip ended happily, when Kirin was mated to Toshita of Honshu resulting in the deep red-and-white dog, Ch. Shojo of Camplane. Shojo went on to sire Ch. Tisen who gained her title in 1972.

TUEZA

The Japananese Chin has an endearing character, and the breed's admirers tend to remain very loyal to their aristocratic, oriental pets – once smitten there is no escape! One very senior breeder and exhibitor, who is still most active in the breed, is Kathleen Botting. During Kathleen's childhood, her father had been a devotee of the Great Dane, and the young Kath spent her time after school helping to prepare and exercise the dogs. Her other great love was riding, and her Arab hunter Comet and a black gelding named Nightingale were the loves of her life. After Kathleen was struck down with tuberculosis, doctors decided that riding was too strenuous, so both horses were sold and the frail youngster was admitted to hospital for heart surgery.

While recuperating, Kathleen's thoughts turned to dogs in general and to Japanese Chins in particular. She decided that when she was well enough she would go around the shows with the intention of acquiring a good one. Fred Cook was a Papillon enthusiast, an active member and officer of the Papillon Club, and a fellow resident of Berkshire – he was the sole occupant of an island at Caversham Lock on the River Thames. Through his Papillon connections he had inherited the Monamie affix and dogs from Madame Oosterveen, after her death in the late 1940s. He had known both Mrs Mosscockle and Mrs Craufurd, and his tales of their famous Japanese fuelled Kathleen's interest in the breed.

Later, upon Mr Cook's death, Mrs Botting inherited many of the Monamie CCs, papers, dogs and a magnificent painting of Ch. Monamie Michi with his daughter, Ch. Monamie Sadie. Although Mr Cook bred the occasional litter of Japanese Chins, he could not be tempted to part with any of them. Mrs Botting started to visit shows hoping to find a Japanese she could purchase. She met and became friendly with Mrs Craufurd.

In 1968, an advertisement in *Exchange and Mart* caught Mrs Botting's eye. It was for a red and white bitch puppy and, after taking advice from Mr Cook, Kathleen had her foundation bitch. Miss Tovey saw her when she was an adult and advised Mrs Botting to mate her with Mrs Eveline Wickham's dog, Joesfolly Little Snuff. The mating resulted in four bitches which gave the Bottings a great deal of pleasure. Mrs Wickham had one of the litter, and the other three were retained.

Birmingham National Championship Show in 1971 was a memorable occasion for the Tueza Japanese. All of the bitch classes were won by homebred Tueza stock, with Tueza Takara gaining the CC, and Mrs Wickham's Tueza Toka taking the Reserve CC. Congratulations came from Mrs Craufurd among others, and she expressed her delight that the Bottings were doing their utmost to improve the breed. Several other Tueza-

bred dogs started making their mark in the ring. Tueza Tan'yu was a big winner, gaining a Reserve CC at Crufts, and Tueza Tanin-No-Kao gave Kath and Alf a lot of pleasure. Mrs Wickham had both Yevot and Weycombe breeding behind her stock, and she mated Toka to Joesfolly Little Lad. From this mating came Mrs Dolly Gessey's Ch. Joesfolly Little Tomboy and Joesfolly Little Buttons, who in turn was the sire of Chs. Joesfolly Little Baba Two and Ch. Joesfolly Little Eve. The last time Fred Cook was seen in the ring was with a Tueza bitch that reminded him of the Monamie Chins of yesteryear. Deborah Gaines was the judge and he won the Reserve CC. The bitch never returned to the Bottings, but went to live on the island in the Thames with Mr Cook until she died. Alf and Kathleen Botting tell us that they have many happy memories of their Japanese Chins and the friends they have made in the breed. Mrs Botting still shows her dogs and is one of our most senior breeders and exhibitors who is still actively involved in the breed. She has judged the breed on many occasions, the latest appointment being Crufts 1996.

OTHER WELL-ESTABLISHED KENNELS

Two other kennels have been associated with the breed for over 40 years. Mrs Winnie Matches has owned the breed since the 1940s when she and her late husband lived in Hong Kong. Their first dog was Nipper, a seasoned traveller who accompanied the Matches to Vancouver, Canada and then, some years later, returned with them to England. The journey back to England sounds quite eventful, as they travelled five nights and four days by Canadian Pacific train through the Rockies, across the Prairies on to Montreal, then from Montreal to Quebec to board the liner, *Empress of Scotland*. Arrival in Greenock meant six months in quarantine for Nipper, but he took this all in his stride. Nipper lived to the grand age of 16.

He was replaced by Riu Gu Firestep, who lived to the age of ten. Doreen and Gordon Taylor then supplied a young bitch, but she pined for her kennel mate who had been destined for a show career with Gordon and Doreen. The Matches capitulated, bought their second Taydor dog and launched themselves into the world of showing.

A friendship developed with Mrs Rita Evans, who owned the Valevan Japanese and King Charles Spaniels, and Valevan Golden Topaz joined the Matches family. She too lived to a good age, never losing her beautiful colouring.

Winnie's daughter Jennifer is now a Championship Show judge of our breed, and both mother and daughter have an undiminished interest in the Japanese Chin.

CROSSGATE

Peggy Searl (formerly Miss Hodge) is one of the best known personalities in the Japanese Chin world. Peggy was fortunate enough to work with the Riu Gu Japanese Chins as a young woman, and her love of the breed has remained constant ever since. Peggy's marriage to Eric in the 1960s brought another convert into our ranks, and together they campaigned and owned some of the top winning dogs of their day. Peggy's foundation stock came from Mrs Craufurd and, despite the fact that Peggy bred the foundation bitch of

the Alstella kennel, the first Crossgate Champion was not homebred. Hillsmark's Ki Yuki, sired by Ch. Tare Da of Riu Gu out of a daughter of Ch. Momus of Riu Gu, was bred by Mr and Mrs Joe Smith in Scotland and proved to be a wonderful addition to the Searls' household.

Yuki gained her title in three straight shows under three great judges, Mrs Jagger, Mrs Tarry and Mrs Alexander. She came into season the day she won her third CC, so Peggy retired her for a litter. At one time, Eric and Peggy owned five generations of Crossgate Japanese who were all descended from Yuki.

Their next Champion was Eric's Xerxes of Crossgate, who gained his title in 1971. He too was basically Riu Gu-bred and his breeder, Mrs Fanthorpe, showed his litter brother Kogato Bushi with some success. He won two CCs and was Group No.2 at Birmingham Dog Show Society Ch. Show in 1970.

On Mrs Craufurd's death, Ch. Nyorai of Riu Gu went to live with Eric and Peggy. At the time he was ten years of age, but he quickly settled in with them and lived until he was over 14 years old. The 1970s saw Crossgate Xultan exported to the Netherlands, where he made a great impact on the breed. Crossgate Xipper was shown with success and, when mated to Peggy's Gorsedene Stephana, he sired Ch. Crossgate Xclusive. Xclusive was then mated to his grand-dam to produce Xuberant. She was purchased by Ann Francis and is the dam of Mr and Mrs Millar's Ch. Addislea Yakkitty of Turnlaw. Peggy has judged the breed on many occasions, including both Crufts and the Club Championship Show held in 1995 to celebrate the centenary. Over a great

many years, the Searls have given sterling service to the Japanese Chin Club and Peggy is currently the club's president – a richly-deserved honour following in the footsteps of some of the great names in the breed.

GORSEDENE
The Gorsedene affix is one of the best known in the breed. Lilian Davis was chairman of the Japanese Chin Club for several years. Lilian's interest in pedigree dogs was lifelong. As a young woman in pre-war days, she had bred and shown Chow Chows with considerable success. However, it was not until Lilian and her husband Ed retired from their pharmacy business in Derbyshire and moved to Surrey, that she was really able to devote her time to breeding and showing dogs.

The Gorsedene prefix was first registered in 1955, and initially graced several top winning Cavalier King Charles Spaniels and Griffons. As so often happens, a Griffon breeder was attracted

Lilian Davis bred some top-class stock which was to have a great impact on the breed. Pictured is Mr and Mrs Wollen's Gorsedene Taiko, winner of two CCs.

to the Japanese Chin, and our breed very quickly became a firm favourite with Mrs Davis. Her initial stock came from Miss Tovey and Mrs Stella Reeves, and it was from the Yevot kennel that Lilian

Ch. Sternroc Cho Cho of Gorsedene.
Photo: Thomas Fall.

Lilian Davis' Group winning Ch. Gorsedene Hirohito of Yevot.
Photo: Diane Pearce.

purchased the Gorsedene foundation stud, Gorsedene Hirohito of Yevot. Miss Tovey, we suspect, probably felt that he was too large, but Lilian had a lot of faith in him and campaigned him to his title and to the reserve spot in the Toy Group at the Three Counties Championship Show in 1970. Hirohito was to have a remarkable impact on the breed.

Pamela Cross Stern bought the bitch puppy, Sternroc Cho Cho of Gorsedene, from Lilian. Cho Cho subsequently became the breed record holder in her day and, when mated back to her sire, she produced the foundation stock of the Sternrocs. Although Lilian did very little exhibiting, Jeanette, Kirei and Kotei all did a fair amount of winning. Kotei, in particular, was in demand as a stud and many other breeders and exhibitors took advantage of Lilian's flair as a breeder of sound, typical stock. Gorsedene Okami was one of the leading stud dogs of the early 1980s, despite the fact that he was used infrequently. When used by Mrs Reeves on Alstella Elfrida San, he produced one litter which contained two Champions and a third bitch who was a CC winner and unlucky not to gain her title. Another mating produced the CC-winning litter brothers, Gorsedene Taiko and Tassha. Okami's litter sister, Oshima, was acquired by Miss Tovey and was the dam of the last Yevot Champion, Miyako. The brother and sister, Gorsedene Cyrus and Stephana, both produced Champion offspring, while one of Lilian's last litters contained Ch. Gorsedene Kosho of Barklots whom Tom Mather bought as a puppy.

VALEVAN
Rita Evans, who owned the Valevan

Japanese Chins, was a great friend of Mr and Mrs Davis. Rita did so much to promote the breed. The Japanese Chin Club profited from her help for many years, and she was always willing to assist wherever she could. The *Year Book* flourished under her editorship, and she spent many hours making sure that it was a publication to be proud of. As club chairman, she went out of her way to make new members feel welcome and, behind the scenes, she did a great deal of work for dog rescue. The Valevans were campaigned fearlessly both in the UK and Eire, and Rita would often enter very large teams of both King Charles Spaniels and Japanese Chins at almost every show. In the UK, her best-known winners were probably Valevan Princess Chiko, the red-and-white CC-winning bitch, and Koke of Gorsedene. In Ireland, Rita's friend Theresa O'Keefe Horgan campaigned both Valevan Sherri Lanka and Valevan Prince Sachi to their titles. Rita had the honour of judging the breed at the Crufts Centenary Show in 1991, and drew a superb entry. Sadly, she died in 1992 after losing her battle against cancer.

VINOVIUM
Margaret Jagger built up this influential strain of Japanese Chins which achieved worldwide recognition for the Vinovium affix. Mrs Jagger was already a knowledgeable and successful breeder of Cairn Terriers, having owned or bred some top-class stock which included Int. Ch. Vinovium Graham and Ch. Vinovium Pledwick Tiger. In Chins, her first significant winner was Whitethroat Sawayaka, born in 1963. Sawayaka, when mated to Mikami of Yevot, produced the first Vinovium Japanese Chin Champion,

Yum Yum. She won her first CC at Birmingham under Leo C. Wilson, and then gained her title in 1966 by winning the CC under Jean Hopwood at Crufts and a third ticket, under Mrs Warner Hill, at Three Counties. What a foundation Sawayaka proved to be! From the same litter that produced Yum Yum another bitch, Cultured Pearl, won the CC at Bath under Miss Tovey, and then won a second ticket in 1968. Unfortunately, she did not gain her title. A repeat mating produced Vinovium Tatsu, who was sold to Bill Jobson. Tatsu proved his worth as a stud by siring Vinovium Yan Cha, who played such an important part in establishing Ann Francis' Addislea line.

In the late 1960s, Mrs Jagger acquired the black and white Champion, Yakushi Nyorai of Riu Gu from Mrs Craufurd. He, in due course, was mated to Yum Yum to produce Ch. Vinovium Yakita. Sawayaka was also mated to Yakushi Nyorai and this resulted in the Res. CC winner, Vinovium Sokuri, who is behind some of the early Ranella stock. Sawayaka also whelped Vinovium Kenjii, again a most important stud who can be found in the pedigrees of several Champions who gained their titles in the 1980s. Barbara Mills' Hellesveor kennel and, in turn the Sangria and Dunloo kennels, all had lines going back to Kenjii. Mrs Dowson (Makeera), Frank and Sybil Lloyd (Miksu) and Mrs Bennett (Glaisdaleast) all made use of Vinovium bloodlines. Ann Francis said that Mrs Jagger gave her the following advice when she started in the breed: "Riu Gu for heads and Yevot for fine bone."

INTO THE 1970s
As the swinging sixties drew to a close,

registration figures for the Japanese Chin began to climb and, for the first time, the number crept past the 200 mark in 1972. The 1970s saw the loss of some of the older Jap stalwarts, but it also saw newcomers joining the ranks and some of them were to make an indelible mark on the breed.

Life in Britain was very different in 1970; it was possible to rent an unfurnished four-roomed cottage for £60 per annum, while a modern bungalow and kennels set in six acres of land in Berkshire could be purchased for £11,000. The canine press carried advertisements which nowadays would shock the squeamish or conservation-conscious. Shark, whale, venison or horse meat was offered for sale, together with a special delicacy to tempt 'poor doers' – kangaroo in gel!

The breed was allocated only 12 sets of CCs, but frequently made its mark in the Toy Group, such was the quality of the dogs being shown. By 1975, The Japanese Chin Club Bulletin Stud Register gave members plenty of choice. Sternroc Ju-Jitsu, Gorsedene Kotei, Camplane Usui No Sadamitsu or any of four Yevot stud dogs were all at public stud for sums ranging from 7 right up to 12 guineas! When one considers that we now often hear of stud fees in excess of £300 it seems hard to believe that only 20 years have passed.

Let us look at some of the British kennels who have had significant success since 1970.

ADDISLEA
Ann Francis has the distinction of being one of the select few to have done the double at Crufts. This was achieved in

Ch. Addislea Yanusha. Owned by Bryan Mitchell, bred by Ann Francis.
Photo: Thomas Fall.

1980 with her first two Champions, the litter brother and sister, Addislea Yanagi and Yanina. Mrs Conlin Roe campaigned Ch. Addislea Yoshimi, while the great Japanese Chin aficionado Bryan Mitchell piloted the lovely Ch. Addislea Yanusha • to her title. The last Addislea to gain her title was the Millars' Ch. Addislea Yakkitty of Turnlaw.

ALSTELLA

The Alstella Japanese Chins were founded by Stella Reeves. Her first Chin, Kosho of Crossgate, was purchased from Miss M. Hodge (now better known as Mrs Peggy Searl). Kosho, born in 1963 and sired by Ko of Honshu out of Asaji of Riu Gu, was duly mated to Deborah and Tessa Gaines' Gaystock Rising Sun. Two bitch puppies from this mating, Tekko of Alstella – dam of the remarkable Cho Cho – and Yancha of Alstella, were sold to Lilian Davis, and Mrs Reeves retained a dog puppy, Taiko of Alstella.

Taiko was then mated back to his dam to produce Alstella Teaka. Teaka sired nine Champions at home and abroad and, when mated to Gaystock Painted Lady, produced Mrs Reeves' first two Champions, Samantha and Elisa. Photographs of these two bitches portray them as having large heads with wide, well-cushioned muzzles and good width of chest. Mrs Reeves' daughter, Christine

Mesdames Reeves' and Sargant's Ch. Alstella Joshua.

Photo: David Streten.

RIGHT: Samantha Sargant's
Ch. Alstella Angelino.

BELOW: The Alstella kennel has
long been one of the most
influential in the breed. Pictured
(left to right): Ch. Samarra, Ch.
Agnetha, Ch. Longview Tamiko,
Samantha Sargant with Alena,
Ch. Alicia (standing), Tokai
and Ch. Ebony Eyes.

Reeves-Sargent, had always played an active role in the development of the kennel and a repeat mating of Samantha and Elisa in 1973 produced Christine's first Champion, Samarra of Lewisia. Teaka was mated to Mirandus Freesia to produce Ch. Longview Tamiko. Through Elisa came Ch. Alstella Ebony Eyes and Eunice Wordingham's lovely Ch. Lewisia Sareena. Eunice's Champion Wordoaks Marguerite can also be traced back to

Elisa. A bitch by Valevan Harlequin out of Elisa, Alstella Elfrida San, was to play an important part in the development of the strain. When mated to Gorsedene Okami, three bitch puppies were whelped: Ch. Alstella Agnetha, Ch. Alstella Alicia and Alstella Alena who won two CCs.

The acquisition of Navron Zuni and Navron Sadako gave Mrs Reeves and her daughter an outcross through the Japanese stock that was imported by

Derek and Geraldine Smith. Both Zuni's and Sadako's pedigrees are of interest as they carry the bloodlines of both of the Smith's imports, as well as Alstella Tokai, a Crufts CC-winning dog campaigned by the kennel in the early 1980s. Both Ch. Alstella Georgio and the red and white dog Ch. Alstella Joshua are a mix of the established Alstella line with the Japanese outcross. The latest dog Champion to bear the Alstella prefix is owned by the late Mrs Reeves' grand-daughter, Samantha Sargant. Ch. Alstella Angelino gained his title in 1994, and this surely gives the Alstellas a unique place in the history of the breed.

AMANTRA

Diane Fry and her daughter Tracey Jackson have an enviable record as breeders of top-class stock in a variety of breeds. Their Cavalier King Charles Spaniels and King Charles Spaniels were already famous when they turned their attentions to the Japanese Chin. Several Champions carried their Amantra affix, including the litter sisters, Mary Meenan's Eng. and Ir. Ch. Amantra Teo Torriate and Jackie Meakin's Ch. Kichi Kodamo of Amantra. Peggy Lanceley's first Champion, Barabelle Blueanton, was out of Apoco Kisaki of Amantra. Mary Meenan had a number of dogs from the Frys, and these made their mark in Ireland and in England. The first Irish-bred and owned English Champion, the Brittains' Wynnsward Brian, was sired by Amantra Hokusia Tosu.

However, it was a Japanese import, owned by Tracey and often shown by her husband Ian, who was to have the biggest impact on the breed. Japanese Champion Ryusho of Matsuminesow at Amantra was

Eng. Jap. Ch. Ryusho of Matsuminesow at Amantra.   Photo: Thomas Fall.

the first Japanese Champion to come to this country. He had a lovely head with a wide, well-cushioned muzzle and the desired "look of astonishment". Additionally, he had the most marvellous temperament. He sired five English Champions, including the Group-winning Kotaro.

APOCODEODAR

This affix came into being as a result of the partnership between Bill Stevenson (Apoco) and Sylvia Borthwick (Deodar). Both Bill and Sylvia had a long-standing interest in the breed, and both were experienced and extremely successful breeders. The Apoco affix is in many pedigrees of the late 1970s and early 1980s, while Sylvia had bred stock which had been utilised in the bloodlines of many other breeders, including Mr and Mrs Wollen and Miss Tovey.

Their first Champion in the breed was Magic Dragon of Apocodeodar who, together with his litter sister, the Res. CC-winning Dragon Flower, started the Stevensons off as exhibitors and breeders of top-flight Japanese Chins. Magic Dragon was subsequently exported to the Hoobans in the USA, where he gained his title. Their next big winner was Ch. Kelitos Kimono of Apocodeodar. He was bred by Lilian Smith, but his pedigree contained Sylvia's Deodar breeding in the background. Ch. Apocodeodar Paper Dragon won one CC in the hands of the Stevensons, but was then transferred to Bryan Bond and George Farmer – he was to have a great influence on the Sangria kennel.

Bill and Margaret Cartwright's Ch. Naoi Se of Apocodeodar did a tremendous amount of winning and went on to sire Michelle Evans' Ch. Wilmaden Chinka. The red and white bitch, Ch. Apocodeodar Moyah went on to join Molly Coaker's Homerbrent kennel, while Ch. Apocodeodar Sumi was the last Chin to be campaigned by Bill and Sylvia. Bill and Sylvia emigrated to Australia in the mid-1980s and, sadly, Sylvia died in 1989. Just a couple of months after Sylvia's tragic death, Jean Wallhead gained a third ticket with Ch. Apocodeodar Kuku at Merida. Many other breeders made use of Apocodeodar stock and the Stevensons made a valuable contribution to the breed.

BARKLOTS

Tom Mather has shown dogs since he was a schoolboy and, with his sister Sara, was one of the first Bichon Frise exhibitors in the UK. After deciding to try and buy a Japanese Chin, Peggy Lanceley was approached to see if she had anything that might be suitable. Dr and Mrs Lanceley generously offered a young bitch, Serlo Lady Julie of Blueanton. Julie was demanding and would not be left alone for a moment, but she was a born show-off and quickly started winning in both breed and variety competition.

No one could have had a better start in a breed than that given to Tom by his two great friends. Julie won 15 CCs, two at Crufts and a BIS at the Japanese Chin Club Championship Show. She only had one litter but that contained the diminutive red and white bitch, Ch. Barklots Tiger Lily. Lily was sired by one of Lilian Davis' Gorsedene dogs, and a friendship with Lilian led to the purchase of Gorsedene Kosho of Barklots, who gained her title when just over 12 months of age. All of the Barklots live as pets, and Tom's mother Margaret must take the credit for their condition.

In 1986, Brian Conn asked Tom if he would be interested in showing the young

Ch. Serlo Lady Julie of Blueanton.

red and white dog, Sternroc The Airy Fairy. He gained his title that year and this led to Tom showing the Sternroc dogs for Mr Conn. Since 1986, all of the Sternroc Champions, except Pamela Cross Stern's Fabulous Fairy, have been campaigned by Tom Mather.

A new bitch puppy has recently joined the Barklots troupe, imported from Tommy and Anne Botten in Norway. She carries Riu Gu and Sternroc bloodlines, so more breeding may be undertaken in the future.

BLUEANTON

Peggy Lanceley was a breeder and exhibitor of Yorkshire Terriers, but arthritis made presenting such a demanding breed difficult. With Dr Harry Lanceley's retirement from general practice, more time was available to go to shows and neither of them wanted to spend hours sitting at the benches grooming. Both Harry and Peggy admired the Japanese Chin and, after their purchase of initial stock, the Blueanton affix was soon noticed within the breed.

Ch. Barabelle Blueanton won her title in 1981, and that year also won BIS at the Japanese Chin Club Championship Show under the doyenne of the breed, Miss Tovey. Barabelle's brothers, Beaubimbo of Blueanton and Blueanton Banachek, made names for themselves as stud dogs siring Champion stock for others. Both could easily have won their Championships if they had not been such reluctant show dogs.

Blueanton Bally Jo Jo was another handsome dog who was unlucky not to gain his title. He sired some good stock, including Shirley Appleby's Ch. Pomanna

Arkadia Kamu Saki who went on to sire four English Champions. Dr Lanceley's death in 1988 heralded an end to the Blueanton breeding programme, but Mrs Lanceley's next big winner was Ch. Navron Midori. Purchased from Derek and Geraldine Smith as a young puppy, she gained her title in 1990.

Joy Jolley's Group winning dog Ch. Dekobras Magic Dragon.

DEKOBRAS

The Dekobras affix had been prominent in a variety of Toy breeds, most notably Chihuahuas and Australian Silky Terriers. When Joy Jolley decided to turn her attention to the Japanese Chin it was characteristic of her that she would make a good job of it! Her first purchase was a bitch, Heath's Chick-A-Boo – not a show prospect but well-bred, being predominantly Gorsedene breeding through her Wordoaks sire and Valevan grand-dam.

Joy's first litter in 1989 was sired by

Ann Dilley's Ch. Dunloo Desu Ten-Chi. The three puppies started winning immediately. Ch. Dekobras Magic Dragon was the first to gain his title and was, by the way, also a Group winner. His litter sisters, Dekobras Lotus and Dekobras Mimosa, both went on to gain their Championships. Not many people breed three Champions in their first litter. Lotus was mated to Finchfield Oh No at Dekobras to produce Ch. Dekobras Master Kard, who gained his title in 1995, while his litter sister, Easter Bonnet, is also knocking on the door. Joy is an avid collector of antiques, paintings and postcards, and has one of the most extensive collections featuring our breed.

DENSTONE
Shirley Appleby's Denstone affix came to prominence in the mid 1980s. Pomeranian breeders, Mr and Mrs Welsby, had a Lotusgrange bitch they had bought in from Bill and Margaret Cartwright. She carried Riu Gu and Ulvus bloodlines, the latter from a dog Mrs Robertshaw had imported from Sweden. Mated to Blueanton Bally Jo Jo she produced a young dog, Pomanna Arkadia Kamu Saki. The Welsbys felt they were unable to do him justice, and Shirley made a very astute purchase. He won eight CCs in total but went on to sire four English Champions, with more offspring gaining their titles overseas. Ch. Lotusgrange Choleen gained her title here before going to America to join Sharon Lee Fowler.

Mrs Appleby had a red and white bitch bred by Mrs Stuart Spencer. Chasse Celeste was to prove a marvellous addition to the Denstone kennel as she whelped three English Champions when

Ch. Gloval Simply Red. Owned and bred by Mrs and Miss Nicholson. *Photo: Hartley.*

mated to Kamu Saki – the red and white bitches Denstone Daisymay and Denstone Rozalinda, and the big-winning dog, Denstone Pepi.

Celeste was also the dam of Am. Ch. Denstone Just William and Am. Ch. Denstone Domino at Ranella. Winning stock has been sold to other exhibitors. Doreen and Geoff Gornall made up Ch. Denstone Lucinda, while Jean and Tony Dalton campaigned Denstone Perriwinkle of Tojeda to his title. He was BOB at Crufts Centenary Show under Rita Evans.

Homerbrent Syakai was purchased as a youngster, and he too has made his mark on the breed. He gained his title with ease and has sired some exciting young stock. The author judged the breed at Crufts in 1995 and gave a first CC and BOB to a red and white dog owned by Val and Cath Nicholson. Ch. Gloval Simply Red boasts a Denstone dam and he went on to finish 1995 as the year's top winning dog. At the time of writing, the current top winner for 1996 is Mrs Appleby's homebred bitch, Ch. Denstone Tuff Kuki.

DUNLOO
Ann Dilley is yet another person with a good pedigree in the Toy Group before

*Ann Dilley's Ch. Dunloo Desu Omamori:
The sire of five British Champions.
Photo: Foyle.*

a daughter of Riu Gu Kotetsu – to her title in 1990.

FINCHFIELD
This is not a long-standing affix within the breed, by comparison with some, but Brenda Barrett has had enormous success within the relatively short time she has been involved with the Japanese Chin. No doubt Mrs Barrett's expertise as a breeder of pedigree livestock (the Finchfield name has graced scores of top-winning Persian cats) enabled her to establish a strain of Japanese Chins that very quickly made its mark within the breed both in the UK and around the world. Starting with a

taking up the Japanese Chin. A keen student of both pedigrees and bloodlines, Ann spent time researching the breed before undertaking a breeding programme that paid real dividends. Ann's first Champion, Longview Nismi, carried both Riu Gu and Gorsedene lines, and was mated to a dog bred by Barbara Mills, Hellesveor Kimseki of Sangria, owned by Bryan Bond and George Farmer. This mating resulted in Ch. Dunloo Desu Omamori, a stud dog par excellence, sire of five Champions and an asset to any kennel. His first Champion son, Dunloo Desu Taisetsu-na, actually gained his title before his famous sire. Mori's son, Ch. Dunloo Ten-Chi, has played an important part in the establishment of the Dekobras Japanese Chins, while his daughter, Ch. Dunloo Desu Ame, was a most consistent winner, with two Crufts CCs to her credit.

A great admirer of the Riu Gu Chins, Ann campaigned the delightful red and white Lotusgrange Serenade of Dunloo –

Sharon Lee Fowler of Michigan USA has imported some top-winning stock from the UK. Am. Ch. Finchfield Fujisan, bred by Brenda Barrett, is the sire of eight Champions.

Sangria bitch, and using some of the best-known stud dogs, the first Champion to carry the affix was Mrs Coaker's Finchfield Kenichiro at Homerbrent. He was out of a homebred bitch and sired by Homerbrent Kazari. Mrs Gooding used Kazari on Finchfield Dragonfly to produce Mrs Hurdus' Ch. Dovecliffe Debutante. Kazari came up trumps again to sire George Farmer's and Bryan Bond's Ch. Finchfield Standing Ovation of Sangria. Although Mrs Barrett does occasionally show her dogs, most of her stock is sold to other exhibitors or exported. Altogether there have been 12 Finchfield Champions and, as recently as 1996, the author made Irish Ch. Finchfield Kazzi Best in Show at the Irish Japanese Chin Club Show. This show was held in conjunction with a major Championship Show in Eire, and Kazzi went on to top the Toy Group.

GLENDYKE
Joyce McFarlane's first Champion gained her title in 1988. Ch. Chasse Over The Rainbow at Glendyke was bred by Mrs Stuart Spencer (now Mrs Marjolin). She was mated to Ch. Sangria Eclipse to produce the kennel's second Champion, Glendyke Magic Rainbow. Joyce's daughters, Mrs Sandra Boyer (Ellinghurst) and Linda McFarlane are both keenly interested in the breed, and both were talented junior handlers before progressing to adult competition.

HOMERBRENT
Many newer exhibitors will not realise that Molly Coaker's involvement with the breed spans many years. Although the Homerbrent affix is synonymous with the Cavalier King Charles Spaniel, it is one of

Molly Coaker's homebred Ch. Homerbrent Kimi: One of the most influential sires of the 1990s.

Ch. Homerbrent Ningyoo, owned and bred by Molly Coaker.

the oldest affixes within our breed and Mrs Coaker is one of our most experienced breeders and exhibitors. A litter in 1971 from Kisaki of Chinchivi, sired by Ch. Nyorai of Riu Gu, produced Homerbrent Mikoto of Tragband who was sold to Andrew Brace. Mikoto was

*Ch. Vanistica Astu: BIS at the 1995
Japanese Chin Club Centenary Ch. Show.*

shown in the UK by Andrew before being
exported to Mrs Sigfridsson in Sweden,
where he made his mark as a sire.

Homerbrent Nikko was from the same
mating, and she proved to be quite an
influence on the breed in the late 1970s
and early 80s. Sangria Spring Fever was
mated to Ch. Zanerush Hasha Leeda to
produce Homerbrent Spring Fancy. She
returned to the Sangria kennel to be
mated to Hellesveor Kimseki of Sangria to
produce Sheila Vincent's Homerbrent
Kiko of Yama, the first Japanese Chin
Champion to bear the Homerbrent affix.

In 1986, Bill and Sylvia Stevenson made
up the red and white bitch, Ch.
Apocodeodar Moyah. She was
subsequently sold to Mrs Coaker and
mated to the Wollens' Ch. Ranella
Donovan. This mating resulted in the
Group winner, Ch. Homerbrent Syakai,
who is owned by Mrs Appleby and was
handled by Geoff Corish.

Homerbrent Kazari has sired three
Champions, two of them for Brenda
Barrett. Ch. Finchfield Kenichiro of
Homerbrent was campaigned to his title
by Molly, before joining Peter van Baaren

in The Netherlands. Another Ranella stud
dog provided Homerbrent with their next
Champion. Ch. Homerbrent Kimi
(Ranella Dillon x Homerbrent Koosen)
has proved to be a big winner for the
kennel but, more importantly, he has
sired some terrific stock including Ch.
Vanistica Atsu and his litter brother, the
Dutch Ch. Homerbrent Vanistica Akira.
Atsu won BIS at the Japanese Chin
Club's Centenary Show in 1995, under
the renowned breed specialist Peggy
Searl. Akira has sired stock which is
currently winning well in the USA.

1993 was a good year for the kennel, as
Kimi gained his title and the homebred
bitch Ryoryo won her third CC. She is by
Ch. and Jap. Ch. Ryusho of
Matsuminesow at Amantra, out of
Homerbrent Koosen. 1995 saw two more
new Champions for the kennel. Molly had
mated Ryoryo to Kimi to produce Ch.
Homerbrent Ningyoo, and the dog
Amantra Ryou of Homerbrent – a full
brother to Ch. Amantra Kotaro of Sangria
– gained his title. Mrs Coaker is an
enthusiastic exhibitor who travels many
hundreds of miles each year from her
home in Devon to show the dogs. This
dedication, coupled with her knowledge
of the breed and her expertise as a
breeder, should ensure that the
Homerbrent kennel will remain a force to
be reckoned with for many years.

KO-UN

Margot Ross made her mark in the breed
in the late 1970s with the Junior Warrant
winner, Miksu Moonmaid. Moonmaid
was bred by Frank and Sybil Lloyd, who
have bred some good quality stock over
the years. Unfortunately, she had only a
short, if successful, show career and

Margot's next big winner was Ch. Sangria Sirocco of Ko-Un, bred by George Farmer and Bryan Bond.

Sirocco sired Margot's first homebred Champion, Ko-Un Mariko. Interestingly, she was out of a full sister of Moonmaid. Mrs Ross is one of the best-known faces on the show circuit, as is her husband, Ernest. Until recently, they ran one of the busiest trade stands at most of the major shows. Margot judges our breed at Championship Shows, but still finds time to train some of her dogs to competition standard and is also a judge in the obedience ring.

LOTUSGRANGE

A name synonymous with Pekingese, May Robertshaw has also made a great impression in our breed. One of the earliest Japanese to carry this famous affix was the red and white dog, Lotusgrange Asako of Yevot. He was instrumental in establishing Francine Macey's Franling strain in Jersey, and was used by many breeders of the day. Mrs Robertshaw's first Champion in our breed was the homebred bitch, Lotusgrange Hayari.

May Robertshaw's Swedish import Ulvus Javelin of Lotusgrange.
Photo: Anne Roslin-Williams.

In the 1980s May decided to bring over a Swedish dog, Ulvus Javelin of Lotusgrange. He was not used by British breeders, but had a big influence on the breed as he was used by Mrs Robertshaw on her own stock. He sired the bitch Lotusgrange Chosan of Wilmaden who, when mated to Blueanton Bally Jo Jo, produced Shirley Appleby's influential Ch. Pomanna Arkadia Kamu Saki. Chosan's litter brother, Chodo, was the sire of Shirley's Ch. Lotusgrange Choleen. Lotusgrange Hokori of Highmead was the dam of two Champions for the Dunloo kennel, while Ann Dilley exhibited the red-and-white, Lotusgrange Serenade of Dunloo, to her title. Marjorie Lawrence used a Gorsedene-bred dog on Lotusgrange Tamara to produce Eng. and Am. Ch. Sharlinden Sweet Lorraine At Denstone.

In 1988, the Lotusgrange kennel exported Lotusgrange Thats For Sure to Denmark. He very quickly gained his title in Denmark, Poland, Germany and Holland. Lotusgrange Musoko was a British CC winner before being exported to Sweden, where he gained his title and sired some top winning stock for Scandinavian breeders.

MERIDA

Jean Wallhead was well known in Toy dog circles, principally for her Chihuahuas, before falling for the charms of the Japanese Chin. A long-established friendship with Bill and Sylvia Stevenson, of the world-famous Apocodeodar kennel, led Jean towards the Japanese Chin ring and the acquisition of Apocodeodar Kuku at Merida. A marvellous show dog, she very quickly gained her title and won approbation from both breed specialists and all-rounders alike. In 1990, the black and white bitch, Lavrock Koo-San of Merida, bred by Ray and Diane Jose, gained her title. Ch. Sangria Screen Print followed in 1991, becoming Jean's third Champion bitch in three years – not a bad start in any breed. Jean made up the dog Palteemoor Prince Matsuzo at Merida in 1994.

MUNDEER'S
Janet Chappell's foundation bitch, Miksu Samantha, was bred by Frank and Sybil Lloyd in Derbyshire. In her first litter, to Yevot Ozaki, she produced Ch. Mundeer's Yasako but she was somewhat overshadowed by her younger half-sister, the lovely Ch. Mundeer's Shoji, who won eleven CCs in total. Shoji whelped Mundeer's Kenji, when mated to Hellesveor Kimseki of Yevot, and Kenji sired one of the breed's youngest Champions, Rosemary Lancaster's Mundeer's Hana of Asteran. Hana was a repeat mating of Ch. Mundeer's Senji, who was a great favourite. Mundeer's Koji joined the Wollens' Ranella kennel to good effect. The dog, Mundeer's Chiji, gained his title in 1991. He was out of the CC-winning bitch, Mundeer's Nanji, and had three generations of Mundeer's breeding behind him.

NAVRON
Derek and Geraldine Smith had owned some good quality stock, which had won well without ever really hitting the high spots, when they made the decision to import a dog and a bitch from Japan. Their imports were to have a remarkable impact on the breed in this country and around the world.

Derek and Geraldine Smith's Japanese import Ch. Tatsuo of Matsuminesow at Navron.

The bitch was Fukukohime of Gesshinsow at Navron. She was bred in Japan by Mrs Shizue Fujikawa in 1979, and sired by the Japanese Ch. Kiku No Sukeroki of Hananogisow ex Miho of Hananogisow. The dog was Tatsuo of Matsuminesow at Navron, bred in Japan in 1981 by Mrs E. Matsumara, and sired by Kikuryu II Sei of Suzuyoshisow out of Tancho of Matsuminesow. The Smiths campaigned Tatsuo extensively, and he won a total of nine CCs and gained his title in 1984. Mrs Searl made him BIS at the Club Championship Show in 1985. Miss Tovey gave him BOB at Bath in 1985 and on that occasion his daughter, the Smiths' homebred red and white Navron Titian, won the bitch CC. Derek and Geraldine were thrilled with this win under the doyenne of the breed, and stated that they would always regard Bath, 1985 as their greatest-ever win.

Titian went on to gain her crown in 1985 at the Japanese Chin Club Show under that great lover of a red and white, Margaret Journeaux. Tatsuo was always shown in full coat, immaculately presented and, like all of the post-war Japanese imports to this country, his temperament was superb.

The Smiths embarked on a large-scale breeding programme and much of their stock was exported around the world. Many gained their titles in their adopted countries and, though we cannot list them all, three in particular stand out in our memories: in Eire, Ch. Navron Gushiken, in Holland, World Ch. Navron Omi, and in Finland, Int. Ch. Navron Kai. All three excelled in head and type and were a credit to their breeders.

Other breeders began to take advantage of these new bloodlines. Tom and Margaret Paxton campaigned Navron Yukiko to her title. She was pure Riu Gu on her sire's side, but her dam combined the breeding of the Smiths' two imports. Peggy Lanceley bought Ch. Navron Midori. Like the Paxtons' bitch, she is a descendant of both Tatsuo and Fukukohime. The Ranella and Alstella kennels added Navron stock to their breeding programmes, and Mrs Pauline Khouri based her Sheriko stock on a mixture of established British bloodlines and Navron stock. Pauline piloted the CC-winning bitch Navron Kitaro of Sheriko to many top wins. Derek and Geraldine gave up the breed several years ago.

RANELLA
Roger and Pauline Wollen have been successful Japanese Chin breeders and exhibitors for well over 20 years. Their

Nor. Swed. Ch. Ranella Iamdarci.

ABOVE: Ch. Sharlinden Fumidan of Vival, owned by Mrs E.C. Tappenden, is typical of the stock bred by Marjorie Lawrence.   Photo: Tracy Morgan.

BELOW: Int. & Nor. Swed. Ch. Ranella Bonzai.

record of achievement in the breed is remarkable for a small home-based kennel, where the dogs are primarily pets. Early purchases for the kennel included stock from Miss Tovey, Mrs Pedley (Moordown) and Mrs Craufurd. It was a Riu Gu dog, Bimei (a Yama Kiko son), that gave the Wollens their first Champion in 1977.

Homebred winners soon followed. Ranella Princess Kami was mated to Yama Kiko to produce the CC-winning Ranella Pin Pin, and Jorge Sanchez and Gilbert Kahn's Am. Ch. Ranella Johnny B.Goode. Pin Pin then sired Ch. Ranella Frankie, who became the kennel's first homebred UK Champion. Gorsedene Taiko was added to the kennel and he won two CCs, but the next big winner was Ch. Ranella Donovan. Pauline and Roger admired the Japanese Champion Ryusho and were among the first to make use of his services as a stud dog. Their confidence in him was rewarded, as he sired Ranella Dillon and their first bitch Champion, Ranella Rose Marie. They were out of Ranella Danielle, a full sister to Donovan. Donovan sired Ch. Ranella Jenni when mated to Navron Tu-Tu at Ranella. Tu-Tu provided a further outcross for the kennel as she was sired by the Smiths' import from Japan, Ch. Tatsuo of Matsuminesow at Navron, and on her dam's side had both Japanese and Alstella bloodlines.

Ranella Dillon proved to be a real asset to the Wollens. Molly Coaker used Dillon on Homerbrent Koosen to produce the influential Ch. Homerbrent Kimi. At home, when mated to Paula of Ranella, he sired Ch. Ranella Roxanne, while a mating to Tu-Tu resulted in Ch. Ranella David.

Other breeders have made good use of the Ranella bloodlines. Marjorie Lawrence used David to produce the litter bother and sister, Ch. Sharlinden Benjimino of Vairigoes and Ch. Sharlinden Fumidan of Vival. Margaret and Tom Paxton have used both Ranella Teddy and Ch. Ranella David to produce Champion stock.

Most of the stock bred by the Wollens has been retained by them. However, Stine-Anette Hansen and Ivar Mikarlsen of Norway have had some tip-top stock sent to them by Roger and Pauline. Ranella Bonzai, Delia and Iamdarci have all gained their titles in both Norway and Sweden.

RIU GU

Ch. Riu Gu Fudo. Owned and bred by Mrs E. Craufurd.

The early 70s saw the Riu Gu kennel go from strength to strength. We have already discussed the fabulous Ch. O'Kayama and she, together with her kennel mate Yorimitsu, gained her title in 1970. 1972 saw two more title winners, Ch. Riu Gu Fudo, who went on to win BOB at Crufts in 1973, and Ch. Riu Gu

A delightfully informal shot of Mrs Craufurd at home with the Riu Gu family.

Yama Kaze, who was BIS at the Club Championship in 1971.

The last Champion to be campaigned by Mrs Craufurd was Riu Gu Yama Kiko, bred in the purple by Nyorai ex O'Kayama. He gained his title in 1973 and was a Group and BIS winner. Many considered him the finest Riu Gu ever, and he must have given his clever breeder much satisfaction. Mrs Craufurd died on January 2nd 1976, and she was mourned by her many friends throughout the world of dogs. Her memory will be perpetuated forever through the legacy she left to the breed. On her death, the Riu Gu affix was assigned to her great-nephew David Haig.

SANGRIA
George Farmer and Bryan Bond have

been among the most successful breeders and exhibitors of the 1980s and 90s. These two gentlemen were (like many other Japanese Chin fanciers) very successful Chihuahua breeders and exhibitors before adding our breed to the Sangria kennel. Noted for a high standard of presentation and handling, their dogs have been consistently placed in Group competition and they have been the lucky recipients of the double (i.e. both the dog and bitch Challenge Certificate) on many occasions.

Their first major winner was Ch. Hellesveor Kima-Tommo of Sangria. He was bred by Barbara Mills, who although she rarely exhibited herself, consistently bred some top-quality stock over the years. In the same year that Tommo gained his title, Mrs Ross made up the Sangria-bred dog, Sirocco. Another son of Kima-Tommo gained his title in 1984. Ch Sangria Stormboy only won three CCs, but his first CC with BOB was at Crufts in 1983 under Peggy Searl. His second, also with BOB, came from the maestro, Joe Braddon, at Crufts 1984.

Ch. Sangria Eclipse was a grandson of Stormboy and emanated from a mating that was to prove extremely successful for the partnership. Sangria Storm-Raiser was mated to Ch. Apocodeodar Paper Dragon and whelped Eclipse in her 1985 litter. A repeat mating in 1987 produced the marvellous litter brother and sister, Ch. Sangria Imperial Dragon and Ch. Sangria Screen Print. Eclipse sired the Group-winning bitch Ch. Sangria Paper Lace, and, at Crufts in 1992, this father and daughter couple carried off both tickets. Eclipse won the dog CC at Crufts in 1990 but on that occasion his daughter, Ch. Apocodeodar Kuku at Merida, was

Ch. Sangria Imperial Dragon (left), the top winning Japanese Chin dog of 1990 and BIS at the 1992 Japanese Chin Club Specialty, and his full brother Ch. Sangria Eclipse, a double Crufts CC winner and BIS at the 1989 Japanese Chin Club Ch. Show.

BOB. The next Champion to carry the Sangria affix was a dog bought from Diane Fry and Tracey Jackson's Amantra kennel. Ch. Amantra Kotaro of Sangria was by the Japanese import Ryusho, and possessed his sire's fabulous temperament and lovely head. Two more title winners were added to the kennel's records in 1994. Ch. Finchfield Standing Ovation of Sangria was bred by Brenda Barrett and he too had Japanese bloodlines, while a daughter of Imperial Dragon, Sangria Shooting Star, is the latest bitch Champion for these two clever breeders.

SHERIKO

Pauline Khouri has built up a successful strain of Japanese Chins at her kennels set in the Yorkshire countryside. Her original stock was from well-established kennels, and Mrs Khouri has blended both Japanese and British bloodlines to establish her own strain. 1991 was an excellent year for the kennel. Navron Kitaro of Sheriko was the bitch CC winner at the Club Championship Show,

while two new Champions emerged, both bred by Pauline. Ch. Sheriko Keiko is owned by Ian and Denise Whitehouse and her litter sister is Ch. Sheriko Yoko-Ono. The dog, Alstella Joseph of Exquisanne, was added to the kennel and has one CC. The homebred Sheriko Yancha is a CC winner, while Mrs Reeves-Sargant has the Champion bitch Sheriko Yorkobi at Alstella.

STERNROC

Pamela Cross Stern, together with her partner Brian Conn, have had enormous influence on the breed in the UK. In the late 1960s, Pamela was working in London and went along to Lilian Davis to use a Griffon Bruxellois stud dog. Lilian, at the time, had a litter of Japanese puppies, sired by Ch. Gorsedene Hirohito of Yevot, which caught Pamela's eye. Unfortunately, there was no bitch available. Lilian promised to let Pamela know when she had a bitch by Hirohito, and it was not too long before Sternroc Cho Cho of Gorsedene found her way to

Pamela's London home.

Her impact was immediate. Nora Down gave her a first CC at the age of eleven months at Paignton Show, and she went on to take the breed record for bitches with 16 CCs in total, a record she held until beaten by her grand-daughter, Kiki. Cho Cho was mated twice to her sire. In the first litter, she whelped one bitch, Suzuki, and the second litter produced three bitches, Geisha Girl, San Fairy Ann and Tokyo Rose. Geisha Girl was duly mated to Mrs Craufurd's great Ch. Nyorai of Riu Gu, and three super dogs were the result – Ju-Jitsu, Karate and Judo.

Sternroc Blanco Pantalones, a daughter of Suzuki (when mated to Judo), produced Ch. Sternroc Biki, and a repeat mating produced Ch. Sternroc Chiiki. A dog from this mating, Sternroc Tanoshi, was unlucky not to gain his title, but he sired the fabulous Ch. Sternroc Oska who won BIS at the Japanese Chin Club Show in 1983.

San Fairy Ann was subsequently mated to Ch. Sternroc Ju-Jitsu, and her three litters by him threw Ch. Sternroc Kiki, Ch. Sternroc Tiki and the incredible Ch. Sternroc Dikki. Dikki was the breed record holder, the Dog of the Year for 1981 (all breeds) and the only Chin ever to have twice won Best in Show at all-breed Championship Shows in the UK.

In 1980 the imported dog, Ginzan's Prince Yamadori of Sternroc, gained his title. He was bred by Sigun Carlson in Sweden and was out of Int. and Nord. Ch. Sternroc Ginza. He was shown sparingly in the UK, but sired Ch. Stenroc Yam Sain before returning to Scandinavia where he has played an important part in shaping the breed.

Ch. Sternroc The Airy Fairy.
Photo: Thomas Fall.

The top winning Japanese Chin of all time, and 1981's Dog of the Year – W.B. Conn's Ch. Sternroc Dikki.
Photo: Thomas Fall.

Dikki was used only rarely at stud. To Sternroc Kosho he threw the pale red and white dog, Brian Conn and Tom Mather's Ch. Sternroc The Airy Fairy. Mated to Sternroc Biyo (a daughter of Judo), he sired four bitches: Ch. Sternroc The Fairy Tail, who was campaigned to her title by Jim and Ena Douglas; Ch.

Sternroc The Fairy; the Res. CC winner, Sternroc The Fairy Queen; and Sternroc The Fairy Story. When used by Jim and Ena Douglas on their Carraig Doli, he sired Ch. Carraig Darbi.

Airy Fairy was used twice at stud and, on both occasions, he was mated to his half-sisters. In his first litter to Fairy Story he threw the pale red and white dog, Sternroc The Lemon Fairy. He did some useful winning as a puppy but then decided the show ring was not his cup of tea. The second litter was to Fairy Tail and contained three dogs.

The dogs all three gained their titles, and all three figured in Group competition, with both Ch. Sternroc The Fabulous Fairy and Ch. Sternroc The Fairy Folly winning a Group No. 2 placement, while Ch. Sternroc The Fairy Frolic topped the Toy Group at Driffield Championship Show. Fairy Tail was then mated to her son, Fabulous Fairy, to produce a litter containing a dog and a bitch. The dog was Ch. Sternroc A Fenominal Fairy who, again, figured in Group competition, and the bitch was Ch. Sternroc Fairy Fortune, a Crufts CC winner.

SWIETENIA
Based on the Wirral peninsula in the north of England, Tom and Margaret Paxton first saw the breed at Peggy Lanceley's Blueanton kennel. A pet dog from Peggy was enough to whet their appetites, and they set about buying a bitch they thought would be good enough to show. Derek and Geraldine Smith provided their foundation bitch, Ch. Navron Yukiko, who gained her title in 1991.

Yukiko was by Riu Gu Kiku out of Navron Tu-Tu at Ranella. Tu-Tu's later litters provided two Champions for the Ranella kennel. Yukiko was mated to Ranella Teddy to give the Paxtons their second Champion, Swietenia Evette. A mating of Yukiko to her half-brother, Ch. Ranella David, resulted in Ch. Swietenia Fredrika. Another Ranella dog, Just William, was then used on Fredrika to produce the top winning Chin of 1995, Ch. Swietenia Heather, and her litter sister, Ch. Swietenia Hannah at Ranella.

The Swietenia Chins are all house pets and the Paxtons can rarely be persuaded to part with their stock. Their remarkable consistency is to be commended.

TENSON
The late Mrs Eileen Haig was introduced to the breed through her husband's aunt, Mrs Eileen Craufurd, and it was with Riu Gu foundation stock that the Tenson kennel was founded. Eileen's first litter, by Ch. Riu Gu Yama Kaze ex Riu Gu Ginka, was born in 1973. What a litter it turned out to be! Tenson Uigo was exported to Mesdames Pym and Kay in the USA, and gained his American title by April 1975. Tenson Daku was retained by Eileen and won his first CC in 1975, going on to gain his title in 1976. Tenson Etsu went back to Mrs Craufurd before being acquired by that great dog man, Peter Newman. In Peter's ownership, he quickly gained his title, winning his third CC at the UK Toy Dog Show in 1977, under breed specialist and noted Toy authority Mrs Dorothy Garlick. On that occasion he was handled by Joe Braddon and went on to win Reserve BIS. Etsu was Joe's devoted pet, and Mr Braddon was forced to write in his weekly column for *Our Dogs:* "Just to scotch a wild

An enchanting photo of the Riu Gu and Tenson Japanese Chins: Ch. Tenson Atae, Ch. Tenson Fugi, Ch. Tenson Daku, Riu Gu Ginka, Riu Gu Nimotsu, Ch. Riu Gu Yama Kaze and Ch. Riu Gu Yorimitsu.   *Photo: Thomas Fall.*

rumour, Ch. Tenson Etsu is definitely not for sale, despite the fact that some very tempting offers were made for him. He's the boss dog at Barley Leys and here he remains in charge!"

Daku was then mated to his dam to produce Ch. Tenson Fugi. When mated to a bitch bred by Miss Sully, Camplane Toyo Tama, he sired Ch. Tenson Atae, the CC-winning bitch Tenson Chea, and the Res. CC winner Tenson Amai, who was sold to Derek and Geraldine Smith. Daku was mated to Janet Chappell's Miksu Samantha to produce the big winning Ch. Mundeer's Shoji. The last

Champion from the kennel was the Camplane-bred bitch, Tenson Gaki. Eileen, sadly, died in 1996. She was to have judged the breed at Crufts in 1997.

YEVOT
In 1970, Lilian Davis piloted Ch. Gorsedene Hirohito of Yevot to his title. He went on to take the Reserve spot in the Toy Group at Three Counties that year and, although Miss Tovey considered he was up to size, she must have been proud of the dog she bred. The bitch, Sekki of Yevot, who was sired by Ito of Yevot, gained her title in 1976. Ch. Yevot Nezumi gained his title in 1978. Several Yevots, Yevot Kisaki, Yevot Mitzu and Yevot Kimura, went on to win CCs, but did not gain their titles.

Yevot Hiroshi won BIS at the Japanese Chin Club Show in 1980 and, although he never gained his title, he sired the CC-winning bitch, Yevot Katishi, and one of the top winning red and white dogs of his day, Yevot Akiro. The bitches, Pawnook Narcissus and Yevot Geisha Lady, were both CC winners, and gave Miss Tovey much pleasure. Nezumi died at the early age of seven in 1983 and, for the very first time since 1927, Miss Tovey was without

Ch. Tenson Fugi.   *Photo: Thomas Fall.*

The last Yevot Champion, Miyako.

Photo: Thomas Fall.

A lovely head study of Yevot Kano.

Photo: Thomas Fall.

a Champion in the kennel.

This situation was rectified in 1988 when the homebred dog, Yevot Miyako, gained his third CC. Miyako was sired by Hiroshi and was out of a bitch bred by Miss Tovey's old friend, Lilian Davis. Gorsedene Oshima was a litter sister to that grand sire Gorsedene Okami and, of course, she was line bred to the great Hirohito.

Miss Tovey died on January 3rd 1989. Her dogs were left in the care of her great friend Richard Hall. Just a week before her death, she wrote with news of her eleven Japanese Chins and three Chihuahuas. She was planning a litter from a young bitch she had bought, sired by a Japanese import, and was looking forward to the shows in 1989. She finished by saying how blessed she was to have so many friends, nephews and nieces as well as her beloved dogs. She was a most remarkable woman, a true lady and a great friend to the breed.

BELOW LEFT: Miss Tovey's Ch. Yevot Nozumi.

BELOW RIGHT: Yevot Hiroshi.

Photo: Thomas Fall.

Photo: Thomas Fall.

10 THE JAPANESE CHIN IN NORTH AMERICA

America can justly claim to be the melting pot of the world and, indeed, all nationalities have made their homes there and become Americans. A similar thing has happened in the dog world – except that each breed has retained its own individuality almost completely. I say "almost" completely, because there are variations on a theme.

For example, in presentation, one sees a Bouvier des Flandres with a shampooed, blow-dried coat which is very eye-catching, but does not comply with the coat clause in the country of origin which says: "So thick, when separated by the hand skin barely visible. Coarse to touch, dry and matt." With English Springer Spaniels and Golden Retrievers – to name but two breeds – controversy exists on type between the country of origin and the USA.

So, how about the Japanese Chin? The main difference between the breed in Canada and the USA and the rest of the world (including Japan) is the question of colour. Most countries recognise black and white, and red and white, there being some variations on the term "red" which includes lemon. However, they do not recognise tri-colours. North America does, saying in the Breed Standard: "Either black and white or red and white, or black and white with tan points".

It has also been advocated, in the official publication of the Japanese Chin Club of America, that Japanese Chins should, for neatness, have their feet trimmed. This would, however, result in the loss of the desired "pointed look" to the feet, which other countries consider a breed feature.

HISTORY AND POPULARITY
The Chin came into America about the same time as the Pekingese and, for a while, the popularity of the two breeds seemed about equal. Also, the two breeds appeared to attract a similar group of fanciers. From its introduction into North America, the breed was known and registered as the Japanese Spaniel until August 9th 1977, when its name officially became the Japanese Chin.

The Japanese Spaniel Club of America was founded in 1883. It was probably re-formed in 1895 but, in any event, the Japanese Chin Club of America held its Centennial Show in Santa Rosa,

129

California in September 1988.

About the time of World War One, the Japanese seemed to lose some of its popularity. It was a well-known fact that, until modern vaccines became readily available, Chins were very susceptible to distemper and perhaps this had something to do with their wane. Certainly, during the course of the world conflict, it just was not possible for dogs to be transported between countries, so imports were at a standstill.

EARLY BREEDERS

There had been quite a following in the breed in the early 1900s when Mr and Mrs Roger Harrison of New York started breeding Japanese Spaniels. A black and white Japanese import featured in the breeding and they made up their first Champion, a bitch called Okasan. Their second was another bitch, Sama. By the 1920s, the couple had developed a breeding pattern, produced a dominant male line and were using the same sire on different bitches with great success, producing several champions. By the 1930s they were successfully line-breeding.

In those days, it would seem that people did not travel far to use a stud dog. Just prior to World War One, a dog called King was imported from Japan by a Dr Wyland of Santa Rosa and became an American Champion.

PROMINENT BREEDERS 1918-1940

During this period, there was much activity in the breed, and a number of imports came into the country. One must marvel at the journeys these imports made, in those days, to reach their new homes. For many the mode of travel was across the Pacific (by ship, of course), then overland from a Canadian Port to New York. While most of the breeding seemed to be in the Eastern part of the USA, fanciers in California were also purchasing stock from these breeders

Mrs Berendsohn of Brooklyn, New York, had been interested in dogs since childhood and was making up champions from 1914 onward. In the early 1930s, she imported a bitch from Austria, Nagako v Miniatur, who won the Japanese Spaniel Club of America Specialty in 1933, 1935 and 1936. She also imported several from Ineko Shimokawa's Kumochi Kennel in Japan. At one time, Mrs Berendsohn was secretary of the Japanese Spaniel Club of America. She had a lifelong interest in the breed and was an exhibitor for 40 years.

Helene Fruhauf, from New York, established her line from the Kumochi kennel, buying in three dogs and a bitch, as well as purchasing locally from the Eastern States of America. She eventually ended up breeding completely from Japanese lines.

Georgina Cuthbert must surely have been one of the early pioneers, importing from England in 1926. The import was Odana from Mrs K. Stevens. It would appear Miss Cuthbert adopted the kennel name – whether by design or accident – of Keuwanna. Odana became an American Champion and was known as "...of Keuwanna". Miss Cuthbert lived in Pennsylvania, and her prefix is at the back of many old pedigrees. This kennel subsequently showed the Toy Group winner at Westminster Kennel Club, Ch. Keuwanna Titi. In 1935, Mrs M.F. Dilks (could this be the married name of Miss Cuthbert?) imported a dog from

Germany, Omiako v. Schloss Chemnitz, whose pedigree carried the well-known English bloodlines "...of Hove" on both his sire's and his dam's side. Keuwanna breeding was the basis for the foundation stock of several other lines.

Another keen breeder in the mid-30s, Lida Domler, of Connecticut, established her own Domler line and combined it successfully with Keuwanna, producing a number of Champions.

A CALIFORNIAN BREED LEGEND

Catherine Cross acquired her first Japanese Spaniel in 1923, and was a conscientious breeder/exhibitor of Japanese Chins for 60 years. Quite a record! She bought in from the Durgin kennels and imported Kitsu Of Yevot from Miss Tovey in the UK. Another dog from the same kennel, Am. Ch. Yevot Keiichi Kinkazan, sired four American Champions and one UK Champion.

In the 1970s, Catherine purchased Glaisdaleast Sashi from England, a multi Group winner in the USA, and BOB at the Japanese Chin Club of America Specialty in 1978 and 1979. Catherine won many prestigious events with her stock. After her visit to England in 1973, she wrote: "the English breeders are breeding to the Standard, not asking that the Standard be changed to the type they are breeding. It has been said that the English are better dog breeders than the Americans. They are certainly breeding better Japs." She went on to list some of the advantages the English had: "easier access to good stud dogs (distances not so great); dogs can go on any public conveyance; stud fees low; no cheap champions."

In 1977 Catherine wrote: "The title of Champion in Japanese Spaniels has fallen into disrepute. This is due to poor specimens being exhibited, combined with a judge's ignorance of the Breed Standard. In many cases the judge is faced with choosing the best of the worst. When this happens the judge should withhold the blue ribbon and serious breeders must applaud his decision." I think this has been true all over the world. It takes a brave judge, with the best interest of the breed at heart, to withhold.

Catherine died in 1986, and it was a fitting memorial to her that Ch. Cross Genghis Khan, whom she bred, won Best in Show at the Centennial Show of the Japanese Chin Club of America. She was California's 'First Lady' of the breed. Through her, interest in Japanese Chins increased in the State.

IMPORTANT MODERN BREEDERS

ROBWOOD

The Brewsters, mother and daughter, Mary and Sari (later Tietjen), were well into the breed and stocked up on UK imports, bringing in no less than twelve in the early part of the 1950s. They chose to import from well-known kennels in the UK, selecting Margaret Journeaux's Navy Villas kennel, on Jersey in the Channel Islands. From her they bought in Yola Of Navy Villas, Yu Shee and Kume, litter sisters, and also Sooty. From Mrs Craufurd, of Riu Gu fame, came O' So Sweet, Pavonia, Zephyr, Silvius, Sweetheart and Caligula, all "of Riu Gu" From Miss Jameson came Puffin Of Redcedars and from the Oudenarde kennels of Miss Hamilton and Mrs Temple, Oudenarde Michiki.

Am. Can. Ch. China Doll Taiyo Maid For Me: Winners Bitch, Best of Winners and Sweepstakes Winner at the Japanese Chin Club of America Specialty 1991, aged 12 months.
Booth Photography.

Am. Ch. China Doll's Sweet Baby Jane (Am. Ch. Finchfield Fujisan – Eng. Am. Ch. Sharlinden Sweet Lorraine Denstone).
Booth Photography.

Am. Ch. China Doll Tashi Made In England at Takashi, owned by Marivn and Mavis Hussey.

All of these imports gained their American titles and many had the Brewsters' "of Robwood" affix added to their names. It is interesting to note that Navy Villas and Redcedars, in particular, were renowned for their red and white Japs and, indeed, Mrs Journeaux is still breeding both colours. These imports gave a boost to the Robwood gene pool and, clever breeders that they are, the Brewsters produced many Champions and some lovely stock. Incidentally, it is not surprising that the Brewsters imported heavily from Riu Gu as, just after the time when distemper was rife in the Riu Gu kennels, the Robwoods helped to put them back on top.

SHOW SUCCESS
In 1966, the International Show in Chicago had seven Japanese Chins entered and the famous American judge William Kendrick made Mrs Michael Pym's Ch. Laurel Ridge Timi Tennoo BOB. He also went BOW at Westminster that same year. Winners Dog in Chicago was Japps Beauty Little Star, a Swedish import owned by Rose Petrowsky. There was more than a nucleus of famous bloodlines, many inter-related, from which breeders could choose, and many did! With other imports from England, Sweden, New Zealand and Germany, like the melting pot for the human race, America offered great scope to those who wished to try and 'mix and match' in their quest for the perfect Chin.

Gilbert Khan, now an International judge of the breed, who has the honour of judging at Westminster in 1997, and Jorge Sanchez probably came the closest to this goal with the mixture of bloodlines when they bred Am. Ch. Cary Grant Of

Am. Can. Ch. Shannon's Janlar Rikkio. Bred by Rosa Yokopenic, owned by Jane Pearson. Photo: Steven Ross.

Am. Ch. Shannon's Edo at Epitume.

Holiday House, whose background combines the best of English, American and Canadian bloodlines. Two of their imports, Gaystock Rose Aglo and Ranella Johnny B. Goode, both from England, also feature strongly in Cary's pedigree. Rose went BOB at the East Coast Specialty in 1977 and Johnny was

Am Ch. Cross Loo Kei Mei, Am. Ch. Yevot Keiichi Kinkizan and Am. Ch. Adji Ta Tor.

Winners Dog at the same show. After Jorge died, Gilbert continued to breed and show and has successfully brought out other carefully bred dogs to win their titles. He is currently campaigning Ch. Charing Cross Chindiana Jones.

BLUEMARC
Beulah Koontz Munday has had a remarkable career in dogs. In the early days, she had Pekingese, Scottish Terriers and Borzois. She then took on a boarding kennel and got her professional handlers licence in 1956. With such a background it is no wonder she made her mark on Japanese Chins. Under her Bluemarc affix she piloted many Chins to their Championship. One of the most famous, Ch. Bluemarc's Hojo, whom she owned in partnership with Stewart Ailor, won BOW at Westminster 1970, BOB at the same show in 1972, was top winning Jap in 1970, '71 and '73 and was top producing stud all breeds 1972. He also did some good winning at the Club Specialties from 1970 through to 1972. His breeding went back to the Gailinga line of Mrs Koski in Ontario, and was combined with quite a bit of Honor Guard breeding. This was a favourite combination which Beulah used many times.

FAMOUS NAMES
Honor Guard was the trademark of Yvonne Steiman from Massachusetts. In turn, she used a hefty dose of Gailinga in her breeding programme. Her stock featured strongly in the pedigrees of other well-known breeders – Beulah Koontz Munday, Charmalee Cookingham and Jari Bobillot, Dr Theodore Gorfine (past president of the JCCA), and Donna Hensley, to name a few.

Mrs Michael Pym was a pillar of the breed spanning a great number of years. She was a great ambassadress, travelling and talking to Chin breeders in several countries and had a wealth of information to impart. She was a familiar sight around the breed ring at Crufts and other UK Championship shows

In 1952, Nelda (Billie) Davis of California exhibited her first Japanese Spaniel at the Long Beach Show. Her affix Nel-Da is at the back of a number of old pedigrees. She made up a number of Champions and her combination of Ch.

Nel-Da's Toi Toadi San and Cross Popeaea was so successful that she repeated the mating.

In the 60s and 70s there was a great deal of interest in the breed, and many new fanciers turned their attention to Japs. Mrs Sloan from Gardena, California, did quite a bit of breeding and showing: the professional handler, Mitch Wooten, piloted several of her dogs to their Championships. Jari Bobillot was a well-known breeder and exhibitor from the 1970s on, sometimes in partnership with various people. In fact the combination of Jari, Joyce Boccia and Mary Walsh, stretching across the country – California, Oregon and New Jersey – and incorporating Ur-Chin and New Joy lines, became a most successful partnership.

John and Faith Milton have been among the top successful breeders for many years. Each started in their own right. Michael Pym and Beki Brandon were instrumental in helping Faith (nee Barranco) get a foothold in the Chin fraternity. In fact, she purchased her first Jap in 1972, Jo-Fa's Shesa Keiko Tu, bred by Mrs Michael Pym, and the bitch became Faith's first Champion. During a visit to England in 1981, she purchased Riu Gu Chiseki. In the 1970s John Milton was also successfully producing Champions in the breed. It is not surprising that when these two clever breeders married they went from strength to strength. The number of Champions they have produced during the last 25 years, under their Huang Kung prefix, is too numerous to list. However, one of their best-known dogs was the much travelled NZ Am. Mex. Intl. Ch. Miki Of Shimogamo, bred by Mary Newton, of New Zealand. Miki was not only a great show dog but a very potent sire too. The couple have also imported from Belgium, and from the Netherlands they purchased Tora v Senzai Shu, bred by Margret Steinmeijer-Wagner. Tora became an American, Mexican and International Champion, and won the Stud Dog Class at the JCCA Specialty in 1996, handled by his breeder. Still a puppy as we write, one of the latest to be campaigned by this formidable duo is Huang Kung No Niko Niko. John Milton was, at one time, secretary of the Japanese Spaniel Club of America.

THE GOLDEN SEVENTIES
Several up-and-coming kennels appeared during this period. Overseas travel was becoming easier and less expensive, and holidays abroad meant that people interested in dogs would make sure their visits coincided with some of the larger dog shows. It also gave them an opportunity to call and see various kennels. This, in turn, created the urge to bring back new stock and, as a result, quite a number of imports arrived. For many years the AKC would not register any dog imported direct from Japan. They would not even register one that was imported from any other country if it had a Japanese dog in its pedigree up to the third generation. Dr Theodore Gorfine, president of the Japanese Spaniel Club of America in the 1970s, who made up several Chin Champions and later became a judge, travelled to Japan in 1972. As a result of this visit, he asked the AKC why it would not recognise pedigrees of imported Chins from Japan. He was told that at that time there were three kennel clubs or dog organisations which wrote pedigrees in Japan and, until

they became one and had the same pedigrees, the AKC would not recognise any of the dogs from Japan. This, of course, has changed within the last few years.

The three top-winning Japs in 1973 were Ch. Bluemarc's Hojo with three Group 1 wins, owned by Beulah Koontz; Ch. Tigi Tama owned by Theodore Gorfine and G.L. Davidson; and thirdly Ch. Alexander's Kibo Shen, owned by Fay Skinner and R. Brandon.

THE INFLUENCE OF IMPORTS

The following charts show the impact well-chosen imports made.

1976
1. Eng. import Am. Ch. Sternroc Kyoto. Owned by Isabell Quillen. Best in Show West Coast Specialty May 1975. Sired, among others Am. Ch. Jewel Box Magic Dragon and Am. Ch. Huang Kung No Otoashi Of Jual.
2. Am. Ch. Bluemarc's Sonee.
3. Am. Ch. Harmony's Sansho Of Wesleyan.

1977
1. Eng. import Am. Ch. Tenson Uigo. Owned by Mrs Michael Pym. Gained his Bermudan title, Group winner Montreal, Canada 1976. In 1977 won 17 Group placings in nine months.
2. Eng. import Am. Ch. Sternroc Kyoto.
3. Eng. Import Am. Ch. Glaidaleast Sashi. Owned by Catherine Cross. Won 42 BOBs; six Group placings including 3rd in the Toy Group at the prestigious Santa Barbara Show.

1978
A repeat of 1977 in a different order, with Uigo first, Sashi second and Kyoto third.

OTHER FAMOUS IMPORTS

Throughout the years Japanese Chins from other famous name kennels in the world have emigrated to the USA: Crossgate Xanton, owned by Catherine Cross, winner of the JCCA Specialty Show in Anchorage, Alaska in 1982; Wunwun Of Navy Villas, a lemon and white who won 30 BOBs, numerous Group placings, owned and handled by Lee Troger; Ut-Chu from Hans Sonnenschien, bred by Max Kaats in Germany and imported by Willy and Ursula Hill of Philadelphia; Yevot Yuki, owned by the consortium of Mary Walsh, Jari Bobillot and Susan Hubbard, who also imported Yarmir Enraka; Ch. Ulvus Ling-E-Lang exported by Lisbeth Sigfridsson of Sweden to Donna Hensley, Jadel Kennels; Gorsedene Hitachi went from Mrs Davis to Frances Graham around 1975; and Kinsho Of Yevot – a sable male and the only Japanese Chin to obtain a group placing in 1965 – is owned by Lee Troger and Mary Bingham and won the 1965 Specialty.

Nate and Isabelle Quillen imported from the UK Sternroc Kyoto from Pamela Cross Stern, Lotusgrange Little Treasure from Mrs Robertshaw, and Glaisdaleast Satin-Obi from Mrs Bennett – who also exported Sashi to Catherine Cross and Hina to Mrs Sloan. The Quillens' dogs were handled by Bill Trott who, when this kennel broke up due to very unfortunate personal circumstances, became the owner of Kyoto. Mrs Michael Pym brought in several dogs from England, including Shaunvalley Jasmine from Frank Brown, which she co-owned with Mrs Harold Kay, and Vinovium

Yakita, based on Riu Gu and Yevot lines and bred by Mrs Jagger. Surely the best-known of her imports, however, was Tenson Uigo, bred by Eileen Haig, the niece by marriage of Mrs Craufurd. Uigo's pedigree was pure Riu Gu, out of a bitch Mrs Craufurd had given to Eileen, Riu Gu Ginka. Uigo had a fantastic career in the USA, winning multiple Groups and also gaining his titles in Canada and Bermuda.

Stephen Poltera brought in Ito Of Riu Gu, who gained his Canadian title, and Peter Pan Of Navy Villas. It was Stephen who advocated that colours be written on every pedigree.

Kyomei Sayonarah went to America with his breeder Yvonne Sanderson of New Zealand, who presented him to Mary Walsh with whom she stayed during her visit. It took a while for his registration to clear with the AKC, but it finally did. Lucien Collins co-owned him with Mary and campaigned him to his title in five months.

ALASKA'S FIRST CHAMPION
Mike and Carol Benson had the distinction of making up Alaska's first Champion Chin, Ch. Mi Keys Ohki Doki who also won a Toy Group in that state. The Bensons have continued breeding for quite a number of years and, much more recently, made up a Sangria import. At one time, Michael was president of the Chin Club and also held the office of editor of the club magazine *Chin Chit Chat*.

CONTINUING TO THE MILLENNIUM
Vera and Leland Schenck, of California, were well-known breeders of Japs in that

Am. Ch. Cary Grant of Holiday House.
Photo: Ashbey.

Am. Ch. Charing Cross Quest-Chin-Mark.

state in the 1980s. Their Japanese Spaniels featured in several movies including *The King's Thief* and others about court life. They were also in demand for television appearances.

Rosa Yokopenic purchased her first Japanese Chin in 1984. Others quickly followed and Audi's Kismet O Shannon became her first Champion, going on to produce several more champions for her,

Am. Ch. Charing Cross Chindiana Jones.

Am. Ch. d'Lohr's Beetle Juice Yin Sing (with kennelmate). Photo: Kernan.

notably Am. Can. Ch. Shannon's Bust 'n Loose, who gained his American title in four straight shows and went on to win several Group placings – always owner-handled. Rosa has bred 12 or more Champions in the last nine years, and is one of a selective band of breeders who only breeds a litter when she wants something to show. Her latest 'star' is Am. Can. Ch. Shannon's Janlar Rikkio, whom she bred and now co-owns with Jane Pearson.

The Tosaho Chins were owned by Tommi Hooban whose import from the UK, Amantra Kei Sato, was the kennel's foundation stud. Tommi's daughter Sandi imported UK Ch. Magic Dragon Of Apocodeodar, who soon gained his American title. Under the Tommi-Sans prefix, their Tommi-Sans Tuink-Ling, who became an Int. and Nord.. Am. Dk. Ch. de Nantes '86, was owned by Pekka Jappinen of Sweden, where he also won the Japanese Chin Specialty Show in Stockholm. Another from the Amantra kennel to find its way across the Atlantic

was Amantra Painted Dragon, imported by Mary Brandsford of the Makami affix.

Mary Fitz-Patrick Netz, from Hawaii, took time out to visit Chin kennels in the UK and several other countries. It was with her that Riu Gu Bimyo, originally purchased by Dr Dennis Maher of Australia and holder of both Aust. and NZ titles, spent the last of his days, at the same time achieving his Am. Championship.

Three Sangria imports have gone to Jane Aynsworth, known for her Ukiyo Chins. In recent years, Sharon Fowler imported several dogs from Shirley Appleby of the Denstone affix in the UK. A change in family circumstances caused Sharon to drastically reduce her stock.

The Takashi Japanese Chins of Marvin and Mavis Hussey in Oregon started some ten years ago. The Husseys have based their breeding on English lines, trying to keep them pure, and not mixing with any American dogs. Their first show Chin, Am. Int. and Ntl. Ch. China Dollkato Son Of Sakisu, goes back to

Dunloo and Pommana breeding.

One of the most recent Champions to be campaigned in the East is Ch. Kaminari's Kubla Khan, bred in the purple by Frank Cutler and Benjie Speight out of Ch. Kaminari's Lili Of Cross by Ch. Cross Genghis Khan

An exchange of bloodlines occurred recently between Barbara Vallance who imported Raikon Vom Schloss Orlanda from Christa Franzen in Germany. Orlanda has already obtained his first major from the 6-9 month puppy class. A red and white bitch puppy, Miyagi's Sure To Be Brandy, has gone from the Vallances to Frau Franzen, where it is to be hoped she will soon be making her mark on the European circuit.

Am. Ch. Langcroft Black Tie Affair.
Photo: The Standard Image.

KENNEL NAMES
When tracing through pedigrees it helps to know to whom kennel names and affixes belong.

Affix	**Owner**
Jo-Fa	Faith Barranco
New-Joy	Joyce Boccia
Vip	Iris Paulus
Wunsum	Charlamlee Cookingham
Aver-Har	Avril and Harry Waterhouse
Bluemarc	Beulah Koontz Munday
Chosun	Rebecca Brandon
Chisai	Dixie and Bob McCulloch
Tosaho	Tommi Hooban
Huang Kung	John and Faith Milton
Makami	Mary Brandsford
Jadels Kennels	Larry and Donna Hensley
Yellocro	Gregg Bartoshuk
Ca-Mi	Carol and Michael Benson
Fayaway	Alice Hively
Chin-Dales	Dale and Vincent Adams
Ukiyo	Jayne Aynsworth
Takashi	Marvin and Mavis Hussey

A BOOST FOR REGISTRATIONS

Registrations started to increase in 1965, with 250, compared to 233 in 1964. In Obedience, six Japs finished their CD degree – an all-time high for the breed in the discipline until then. In 1965, twelve Champions finished in 1965, compared to five the previous year. There was only one group placing in the breed in both 1964 and '65, won by two different dogs, both English imports and both owned by the same person, Lee Eric Troger.

It was not until the 1970s that the breed really started to gain in popularity again in the USA, being 87th in line, with 258 registered, in 1970. Since then, registrations of Japanese Chins have increased beyond all bounds.

Figures for 1994 show the Chin listed as 77th, with 1,122 dogs registered out of a total registration of 1,345,941 in all breeds. That same year, 779 litters of Chins were registered. The AKC can amass and collate this general type of information but, because America is so vast and spread out, it is difficult to produce information specific to a particular breed in as much depth as one would wish. Perhaps the advent of the Internet will make this difficulty a thing of the past. It would certainly be a fascinating study for someone to get back to square one, and try and piece the Japanese Chin jigsaw together. It seems that, in the past, there were pockets of fanciers in different areas of the country and these kept shifting from place to place. Many of the earlier breeders were on the East Coast. California then became a hotbed for the breed, while, in the 1990s, the emphasis seems to have shifted to centre on Kansas, Missouri and Texas.

Am. Ch. Tosaho Just So Impressive.
Kurtis Photography.

Am. Ch. Toaho Just So Gorgeous (standing) and Tosaho A Gorgeous Beauty.
Booth Photography.

DOG SHOWS

Sketchy records are available for 1925, when four Japanese Spaniels were entered at Huntingdon Valley Kennel Club. On May 29th 1976, two were entered at the same show. At four All Breed Championship shows held in Pennsylvania and New Jersey in 1996, the numbers of Chins entered per show were four, ten, two and nine – and this with two International Breed Specialists on the judging panel! However, the AKC encourages the formation of local breed clubs to be affiliated to the parent club (Japanese Chin Club of America), and these hold Specialties, often in conjunction with all-breed Championship shows across the States. These Specialties usually attract more entries than the all-breed shows, and exhibitors make a great effort to attend.

In 1948, NOR-CAL held its third Sanction Match the night before the West Coast Specialty and had an entry of 15 dogs and 12 bitches, while the Harbour Cities Specialty, some seven years later, had upwards of 30 Japs present.

From the total numbers of shows and of Japanese Chins entered for 1964/65, the highest number at four shows in 1965 was 27 entries overall and at six shows in 1964 there were 28 entered. 1965 was a better year than '64, having a total of 38 shows and 144 dogs, compared with in 28 shows and 95 entries in 1964. In 1965 entries decreased, with 375 entered compared to 440 in 1964. California dropped in entries from 127 in 1962 to 42 in 1965. However, the number of States with Chins entered in their shows increased in 1965 to 27, from 25 the previous year.

Then we come to the golden Seventies. The NOR-CAL Japanese Spaniel Fanciers' Show in 1976 attracted an entry of 28, compared to the International Show in Chicago that same year which only brought in nine entries. In Salina, Kansas in 1976 there were only two. However, the Eastern Specialty, on October 8th 1976 held in Dulles, Virginia, had over 50 entries. Compare this with the Japanese Chin Club Championship Show held in the UK on October 30th 1976, where 102 Chins made up an entry of 164!

WESTMINSTER CENTENARY
The 100th Westminster Kennel Club Show was held in February 1976 – in those days it was the first 2,500 who sent in their entries who were accepted at the show. It is cold and often very snowy in New York in February, so perhaps it is not surprising that only 19 Chins made it.

OBEDIENCE TITLES
Obedience training and exhibiting for Chins did not really start until about 1949. An ex-Canine Corps instructor held a class in Spring that year and, in the August, Madame Tasselle Of The Orient became the first Japanese Spaniel to win an obedience degree in America by winning her CD. A year later, she gained her CDX title. She won both titles in three shows each and was always very high scoring, usually 195 or better, at a time when judges were very strict. Between August 1949 and November 1972 no less than 23 Japs gained their CD, with five gaining their CDX.

In 1963 Sukie Kun, owned by Mrs James Hoffman (Carol Cowley), gained her CDX award. Others of note (some of them Show Champions too) include: Ch. Kinu CD, also a Mexican Champion, owned by Anne-Marie Kiefer of Los Angeles; Ch. Gailinga's Hisaya CDX; and Ch. Lingel's Ali Iree Kim-Toi CD, owned by Lyle and Mink Linger, of Arizona.

In May 1976, Ch. Kisu's Stars N Stripes attained her CD, and in July 1976 Ch. Kisu's Spotikki Kandoo followed suit. Both bitches were owned by Joanne Sciacca. Spotikki was the first Chin bitch to place in the Group in Bermuda, and completed her CD work in three straight shows. In August 1976, Chinki Sachi, a dog owned by Gloria Letu, gained the

CD title. Aver-Hars Chiisaki Inki Ten, owned by Sandy Batson of New Hampshire, attained CD rating in the record time of just one month! However, no mention of Obedience champions would be complete without including the late Harold Brown's Shin Shi CD CDX: Mr Brown took him through his CDX work totally on hand signals!

SIZE

Every so often there is a discussion in every country about size. In fact, one of my favourite quotes on this subject comes from one of Charles Grinrod's articles (he was one of the early officers of the Japanese Spaniel Club about 1893 in England). Talking about the fashion for breeding tiny Japs he said: "A white Italian rat, painted with black markings, would almost serve the purpose."

An American breeder in the 1970s advocated four sizes of Chin: Giant (14-20 lbs); Classic (6-14 lbs); Miniature (3-5 lbs); and Stirrup Dog, or sleeve dog (under 3 lbs). At this time, the Breed Standard recognised divided classes of seven lbs and over, and under seven lbs.

COLOUR

Colour seems to be a much more controversial subject in America than in the rest of the world, where the original Standard has been accepted without question. The controversy was at its height in the 1970s. It seems that at one time tri-colours were accepted in the ring on the West Coast, but not on the East. In 1978, Stu Ailor wrote in the AKC Gazette: "The Chin is a dog of many colors and we must not penalize a dog because of personal preference. A good Chin is a good Chin regardless of being red and white, lemon and white, brindle and white, tri-color and white or black and white. Color should rank with size as one of the least important aspects of the Chin." It would appear that there were almost equal numbers for and against tri-colours, with some of those in favour using the old adage that 'a good horse cannot be a bad colour'. One of the arguments of those against is: "If you are going to change that part of the Standard, what else are you going to change, and will the breed eventually alter out of all recognition?" Time will tell and we shall just have to wait and see.

CANADA
ORIENTAL IMPORTS

The year that the first Japanese Chin was registered in Canada was 1909-10, according to the Canadian Kennel Club. Interest in the breed, as in many other countries, was interrupted by the First World War, although by the mid-1930s things were picking up again.

NIPPON SAN

Mr and Mrs E.R. Huntington lived in the Orient for 14 years. Originally Bulldog owners, they had to part with them, and their veterinary surgeon gave the couple a young Japanese Spaniel. They fell in love with the breed and gradually acquired more. When the Huntingdons returned to Canada, they brought several Japanese Spaniels back with them and registered the dogs with the Canadian Kennel Club. This stock formed the basis of the Nippon San Kennel.

In 1937 and 1939, Mrs Huntington showed a male in New Glasgow, Halifax and Montreal. She bred one or two litters, keeping several puppies to show. In

Can. Ch. Valleja's Tri N Stop Me CD.
Photo courtesy: Dean Dennis.

Am. Ch. Una-Theodore who whelped six puppies. She kept two of these, who became much-loved pets and went everywhere with her and her husband – even sailing to the Florida Keys, the Dry Tortugas and the Marquesas. She still has a few Chins but is no longer actively showing or breeding.

NAGOYACHIN

Joan Bagnell owned Japanese Spaniels as a child in Nova Scotia, having as pets several of Mrs Guy Watts' dogs. She later acquired the Nagoyachin kennel name from Mrs Watts, bred her first litter in 1970, has made up a number of Champions and is still breeding Japanese Chins.

GAILINGA

In the late 1940s, Lempi Koski started her Gailinga Kennels, producing many Champions. This well-known prefix can be found in many pedigrees. Among her most famous Japanese were Gailinga's Japette, Am. Can. Ch. Gailinga's Rising Sun, and his son, Can. Am. Ch. Gailinga's Fuss-Fuss – a light red and white, known as 'Mitsu'. Mitsu was owned by Jack Quigg.

VALLEJA

Jean Whitford, of Quebec, must be the most prominent breeder of Chins in Canada, and certainly has one of the longest records for interest in the breed in that country. The record holder is, however, Mrs Watts, who is now in her nineties.

A native of Scotland, Jean went to Canada in 1943, started breeding Toy dogs in the early 1950s and, shortly afterwards, pledged her allegiance to

1939, she exhibited five Japanese Spaniels at the Morris and Essex Dog Show (a very famous show for many, many years) held at Geraldine Dodge's estate in Morristown, New Jersey, USA. The judge was Mrs E.H. Berendsohn, who awarded Mrs Huntington's Nippon Mitsui San Best of Breed over an entry of 36 Japanese Spaniels. In 1946, Mrs Huntingdon retired from active breeding and her sister, Mrs Guy Watts of Nova Scotia, took over her breeding stock using the kennel name Nagoyachin. Eight years later, the Huntingdons' daughter Beverley Rogers acquired five Japanese Spaniels from her aunt and, using her mother's kennel name, Nippon San, continued to breed and exhibit.

Six years later, Nippon Arashii San, became the first Japanese Spaniel to gain a Best in Show award in Canada, under the immensely popular and knowledgeable American judge, the late Mr William Kendrick at Barrie, Ontario.

Later, Beverley bred a bitch to Can.

Can. Am. Ch. Ytaaeb's Tanoshii Asi Oto.
Photo courtesy: Alex Smith.

Japanese Chins. She has been a devotee of this breed for the past 40-odd years. Just before his death, Mr Quigg transferred Mitsu and his half-sister, Gailinga's Suzuki Chichi, to Jean and they became the foundation stock for Valleja kennels. Valleja's Mitsu Tori, a result of mating her two original dogs, was the grand-dam of Can. Am. Ch. Valleja' Una-Theodore, who was the top Japanese Chin in Canada in 1975, '76 and '77. In 1995 his grandson, Shades Of Theodore, gained his Championship title.

Jean continued her breeding programme very successfully by combining Nagoyachin and Valleja bloodlines. She imported Valevan Noritake from England (he gained his Canadian title) and Can. Am. Ch. Melmar's Tanyu Of Take Chin from Mary Netz of the USA, thus bringing in Yevot,

Riu Gu and Shimogamo (Australian) bloodlines. It proved an excellent combination, gaining her stock many Group placings and Best in Show awards, and she produced the Number One or Number Two Japanese Spaniels in Canada each year from 1975 to 1994, always handling them herself. As a result of all this, Jean Whitford was awarded various honours, including Pedigree Breeder of the Year and Owner-Handler of the year.

SUCCESS SPREADS
Joan Van Loon, from Alberta, first had Poodles in 1963, but in 1976 purchased her first Chins from Valleja Kennels. All three gained their titles, and she then bought in two sons of Ch. Valevan Noritake, from whom she was able to continue her successful start in the breed.

OBEDIENCE TITLES
Canada has had its share of Obedience Champions, and one of the most prominent exhibitors in this field is Mrs R. Koski, of Thunder Bay, Ontario. Most of her stock originated from the Gailinga's line. She started in the breed in 1948, and has made up double numbers of Champions. Among her Obedience title holders are Can. Am. Ch. Gailinga's Japette CD, Can. Ch. Gailinga's Ba-Bouya CD, and Can. Ch. Gailinga's Hisaya, holder of CDX and American CD.

11 THE JAPANESE CHIN WORLDWIDE

The Scandinavian countries are very closely allied as far as Japanese Chins are concerned. Since quarantine between these countries has been abolished during the last few years, owners are now more easily able to travel to shows and breed their dogs. This is the case, not only in the Nordic countries, but all over Western Europe with the exception of the UK, whose quarantine laws are still enforced.

It is my personal opinion – based on observations made when judging in Scandinavia over the last twenty years – that the Scandinavians are extremely good breeders. I do not confine this opinion only to Japanese Chins. Some people buy a dog and their main ambition is to win with it, and they may acquire another dog for breeding, with little or no thought as to how bloodlines would tie in. Not so the Danes, Finns, Norwegians and Swedes. They think about bloodlines and what they hope to produce when they mate their stock and, in many, many cases, I have seen some superb results. Another thing I particularly like about canine enthusiasts in these countries is that their dogs, of whatever breed, are an

integral part of their family and their life. If they spend the day in the woods or mountains, the dog goes too. Many dogs accompany their owners to work, and it is inspiring to walk round the Kennel Club, and other offices in these countries, and see dogs sitting quietly beside their master or mistress while they work.

Having said this, the Kennel Clubs (and each country has its own Kennel Club, although they all belong to the FCI) are quite strict about the welfare of dogs. Breeders/exhibitors have to belong to the national Kennel Club before they can breed or show, and there are inspectors appointed by each KC to make sure puppies are being properly cared for. But Scandinavian countries are *not* police states – far from it. Caring people go to help breeders out if necessary, and to look after the welfare of the dogs.

Dog shows, too, are very well organised. They are held under FCI rules, as are shows all over Europe, and in some other countries too. It is nearly always mandatory for the judge to give a written critique on each exhibit, and the number of exhibits that can be judged each day by one person is controlled, so that the timing of shows is usually spot-on.

Something else (not universally observed, but a Scandinavian innovation which seems to be catching on in other countries) is the pre-judging of Groups. This saves time and gives the audience a slicker presentation to watch. Having said that, there are usually ten Groups, interspersed with Best Puppy, Breeders' Group and Stud Dog Group. The mechanics of pre-judging are simply that, before the Group is scheduled in the main ring, the judge goes out to the dogs, who are assembled in another ring, and has time to go over each one and sometimes move it. When the dogs enter the main ring, depending on pre-judging time, the judge will either move them all, or send them all round the ring a couple of times, and select several from which to choose the final placings.

Apart from dog shows, Obedience, Tracking, Working and Agility are some other pursuits enjoyed by both dogs and owners.

DENMARK
Countess M. Scheel (nee von Lindolm) of Denmark is claimed to have been the first breeder of Japanese Chins in Scandinavia dating back to the 1890s. She also exported a number of the breed to Germany and Switzerland.

Activity in the breed has never been great, and it almost died out until, in 1966, Liss Andersen, who had seen the breed in Germany and become fond of them, imported two Japanese Chins from England. These were the dog, Shigito Of Yevot, who became a Danish Champion, and Fijihimi, a bitch. Mrs Andersen bred these imports, and mated a son to a full sister, which produced her first home-bred champion, Ch. Yo-Banfas Velo-Wap. In 1973, she purchased Sternroc Ko-Kachi from the UK. He sired two Champions and three CC winners. Unfortunately, Mrs Andersen had nothing to whom she could mate his daughters, so had no alternative but to stop breeding for a while. In 1977 she imported two dogs from Sweden, Borgtunas Poshkin and Koichi Of Akerfjallen, and started again with her successful show kennel. At the World Show in Herning, Denmark, in 1977, the BOB was Yo-Banfas Kochi, sired by Sternroc Ko-Kachi out of Yo-Banfas Taua.

Karin Jensen bought 'Mou', a male from Holland, who became a Danish Champion and also did some winning at Herning in 1977.

Bigarden is the kennel name of Sven and Jetta Mienertz. They have combined Japanese, English, Norwegian and Swedish bloodlines very successfully, as they own three World Winners and two International Champions. Jetta is

Dogs from Countess Scheel's breeding, pictured around 1906.

president of the Danish Japanese Chin Club. There are five or six International shows each year in Denmark.

FINLAND

The first Japanese Chin litter in Finland was bred in the 1930s by Bia Oflund of the No Hana kennel. The dam was a French import. This line came to an end during the war, and the breed became almost extinct. However, in 1966, Paula Kangassalo of Zlazano kennels imported a dog and two bitches from Britain. In the same year, Pitti Sing Of Rosaree was imported by Pirkkpo Pihalja, owner of the Petronella prefix. She was imported in whelp, and gave birth to Finland's first post-war litter.

Until 1978, registration numbers were 3–12 puppies a year, but by 1979 the breed had started to become more popular and 25 new puppies were registered. In 1995, there were about 1,000 Japanese Chins in the country, with 141 puppies registered. The Japanese Chin Club was founded in 1981, and publishes a year book, plus its own magazine three times a year. The club also organises various events.

New blood came into Finland from Britain and Sweden, with a couple of imports from Japan, Germany and the USA during recent years. The imports from Japan, in 1987, were Jap. and SF Ch. Saizo Of Hyuga Kagurason, bred by H. Sonoda of Japan, and owned by R. Amperla of Finland, who also imported Jap. SF and N. Ch. Kotosasa Of Matsuminesow and owned Int. and Nord.. Ch. Habanas Pinnocio.

Paula Kangassalo brought in a Navron dog from England who was also sired by a Matsuminesow dog. This was Navron

Fin. Ch. Mon Aminetten Aythya Ferina.

Kai, who became the most famous Finnish Champion Japanese Chin of all. Mrs Kangassalo also imported Fin. SF Ch. Navron Temajin. Her Harskas Palomino who was by, and out of, two Norwegian Champions, in turn sired several Finnish Champions. In his prime Kai was a lovely dog. I had the pleasure of judging him, and awarded him the Toy Group. Unfortunately, it seems that Mrs Kangassalo has had nothing of his calibre since.

The top winning Japanese Chin in Finland in 1995 was Fin. Ch. Mon Aminetten Bucco Capensis, owned and exhibited by his breeder Paula Kujala. He is a red and white, sired by Fin. Ch. Habanas Anser Fabalia out of Fin.Ch. Habanas Oena Capensis. Breeding some really lovely stock, Paula is certainly a contemporary contender to watch in the Finnish show ring!

NORWAY

Pre-1912, Anna Knudtzon and her daughter Marie owned the Ulleberg kennel in Larvik. It was a fairly large, well-known kennel, housing Toy Spaniels,

Marie Knudtzon and her dogs, pictured in 1913.

Pekingese and Japanese Chins. Anna and Marie showed their dogs whenever they could in Sweden, taking two dogs on the first occasion in 1911 – the English-born 'Jappy' and the Danish-born 'Kito'. Flushed with success, they returned to the Stockholm Show the following year, 1912, with four Chins, and the winner this time was their Imperial Snow (D). These were the first Japanese Chins to be seen in Sweden, and thereafter the Knudtzons exported both Pekingese and Japanese to Sweden. Marie eventually became a judge.

Early this century, there were several other Japanese Chins living in Vestfold. It is thought they were brought to the country by members of the whaling crews, and given as presents to their wives. It was not uncommon for whaling ships to bunker in Japan. As long as they did not go ashore on the way home, these dogs were considered to have served their quarantine period on board ship. Other small Bichon-type dogs were also brought home by seamen. The home port of Norway's whaling ships was Sandefjord.

No Japanese breeders have been traced between the two World Wars, and there is a long gap before there is much else to report regarding the Chin. At the start of the 1970s, Ellen Nythe, who lived near Halden in the south-east of Norway, started breeding Japanese Chins under her kennel name of Yasagata. She purchased two males, one in Tonsberg (Vestfold) and one in Horton, further up the Oslo fjord, where a litter had been born. One of these dogs had Swedish parents, and the other a Swedish sire and a Japanese dam. In 1975, Ellen bought a Chin bitch in Sweden, Ulvus Kamikaze from Mrs Sigfridsson's kennel. Kamikaze was mated to one of Ellen's males, 'Chico', and she kept two bitch puppies from the litter. She then imported Ulvus Majram, a red and white dog, who later became an Int. Champion. She made one further purchase from the Ulvus kennel, a black and white called Yankee Boy.

In the meantime, Pamela Steineger had fallen in love with Japs while visiting her friend Ellen Nythe, and imported Ulvus Extra Twinkle Star, who was later mated to Ulvus Majram. Her next import was Tenson Eika from England. When Ellen could no longer manage her dogs, Pamela Steineger, now owner of Kennel Rossanty, bought them all with the exception of Ulvus Majram, who was so closely related to the bitches that he needed a new range as a stud. He went to Pekka Jappinenen, a

Int. and Nord. Ch. Ulvus Jolly Beggarman.

Finn living in Sweden.

Happily the 'new' Chins settled down well in Oslo, with Pamela's brood of Chihuahuas which she had been breeding for some time. Camplane Tanuki, born in 1977 and inherited by Eileen Haig of the Tenson kennels when Miss Sully died, was sold to Mrs Steineger. He was by Usui-No-Sadamitsu Of Camplane out of Tisen Of Camplane. Pamela refers to him as one of five really great characters she has had in her 40 years of breeding dogs. He put Japs on the map in Norway, and was almost invariably BOB when shown. Pamela kept several of his daughters with her Ulvus/Tenson Eika bitches and, when she needed new blood, bought in a dog from Sweden of Riu Gu/Sternroc and Ginza bloodlines. This, she said, was one of those combinations that look marvellous on paper and turn out to be even better in practice! The dog was Linbackens Spicy Shadow Of Rossanty. Unfortunately, he hated showing so never gained his title, but he proved his worth by siring 15 Champions.

In the early 1980s, Kaja Fygle, who lives in Bodo in the far north of Norway,

bought Ulvus Jolly Beggarman from Sweden, who became and Int. and Nord.. Ch. There were other imports and, of course, stock that had been sold from the Rossanty kennel swelling the entries at shows. I am reminded that, when I judged at the Norwegian Kennel Club's main show in the '80s, I had a class of eight Champion dogs – all beautiful quality – and I said I had never seen a better class of Japanese Chins anywhere in the world.

For the next ten years the breed gained in popularity and many imports came into Norway. Anne Botten, of the High Chin prefix, bought from Sigun Carlson's Ginzan's kennel in Sweden and from England. Mr and Mrs Mikarlsen also bought from Sweden and England. Anne Lise Gulbrandsen brought in NS Uch. Nord. nv 89 Domedikni Nelson from Sweden, combining English and Swedish bloodlines. She, together with the Sandersen family who have the Donald Duck prefix and own NS Ch. Toyosawa's Tooyoo Tama, help to keep the breed to the forefront in Norway, as they are avid exhibitors.

During the last two or three years, there have been a number of English imports from Mrs Robertshaw's Lotusgrange kennels, and the Wollens' Ranella kennels. The tide has turned, and a couple of exports have gone from Norway to England, but have not yet been exhibited. Most exhibitors find they cannot take 'new' dogs to a show without bringing their 'oldies' who just refuse to be left at home. Last year, Belinda Charlotta Of Rossanty, owned by A. Sandersen, was just such a one and was shown in the Veteran Class at 11 years of age – not bad for a Jap!

The three top dogs in the breed in 1994 were:
1. NS Uch. Toyosawa's Tooyoo Tama. Owner/breeder, A. Sandersen.
2. Ranella Iamdarci. Owner J. and S.A. Hansen.
3. N Uch. Pharella's Humble. Owner, J. Oulie.

Sadly, the breed has not retained the popularity which began in the 1980s in Norway – other small breeds have been introduced and become fashionable, mainly the Bichon Frise, but Japanese will always have a small band of enthusiastic fans.

SWEDEN

The 1970s and 80s were years when breeders and exhibitors showed a lot of enthusiasm in the breed. Statistics show that, from January 1st 1970 to December 31st 1979, 878 Japs were born in Sweden and 18 were imported. Contrary to popular belief, the numbers of dogs and bitches was very equal. Of the total number, 441 were dogs (51 red and white) and 437 bitches (53 red and white). Of the imports, 17 came from England and one from Japan. An equal number of eight dogs and bitches were black and white and one of each sex were red and white!

Lisbeth Sigfridsson used the English import Joe's Folly Little Gemshalf very successfully. One of the top winning bitches at this time, Nor. Ch. Ulvus Sagina Bolldottir owes her lineage to him. Litter-sister to this bitch, Ch. Ulvus Selene Venosa, was top bitch 1977 and their full elder sister, Nord. Ch. Ulvus Quanta Essentia, a red and white, did a lot of winning and was Finnish winner in

GB Int. and Nord.. Ch. Ginzan's Prince Yamadoori of Sternroc.

1978. Lotusgrange Musuko, from Mrs Robertshaw in the UK, did well on his first outing at a show in his new country, winning the Cert. and BOB. Yarmir Teishin was another UK import, as was Homerbrent Mikoto Of Tragband, exported by Andrew Brace. This dog sired Sw. Fin. Uch. Ulvus Dragonfly. Mrs Sigfridsson is the owner of the highly successful Ulvus kennel, breeding and making up many Champions and was, at one time, president of the Swedish Japanese Chin Club.

Noomi Samuelson is another well-known breeder and exhibitor, and owner of the Kanemori Kennels. She has made up some Champions and among her early winners were Ch. Kanemoris Geisha and Kanemoris Kyoto. She also brought in Camplane Kappa from the UK.

Ulla Bergostrom's Snoklippans kennel was very successful, breeding several well-known Champions under this prefix. Perhaps her best-known (and one of my favourites) was Int. and Nord. Ch. Snoklippans Su-Ki-Jaki by Int. and Nord. Ch. Ginzan's Butterfly Lion.

Gertrud Claesson (Kennel Saltsjoborg)

was breeding Chins at this time. She imported Joe's Folly Little Gemshalf from Evelyn Wickham, who had the Joe's Folly kennels in both England and Ireland. She also bought in Ajax Of Crossgate from Peggy Searl in the UK. He gained his Int. and Nord. title, and is at the back of present-day pedigrees. However, Mrs Claesson now seems to have gone out of the breed.

Another export from the same kennel, Crossgate Excelsior, went to Kennel Lyckodrommen. Other English imports included: Int. and Nord. Ch. Oudenarde Mikado and Int. and Nord. Ch. Quilichini Of Riu Gu, who went to Lola Reabne's kennel, Japps; Yarmir Obo, who went to Margareta Cederholm's kennel, Av Akerfjallen; and Nikura Of Yevot and Saru Mi Of Yevot from Miss Tovey to Hagar Soderholm of Borgtunas kennel. Mrs Soderholm trained and made up the first Obedience Champion in Sweden, Ob. Ch. Borgtuna's Gim. Playhouse Vinovium Tatsu, later Int. and Nord. Ch., was exported from Bill Jobson to Mrs Lauritzen's Kennel Falloviken. There were several exports from the Smiths' Navron Kennels in England – they had brought in a Chin from Japan who proved a popular stud to their own bitches and, from this breeding, they exported to many countries. Navron Kashira, who ended up with Ninna and Jourunn Winberg of the Harskas Kennels, was actually exported from England to Paula Kangassalo in Finland who sold him on to Sweden.

GB Int. and Nord. Ch. Ginzan's Prince Yamadori Of Sternroc must have been one of Sweden's best-known Japanese Chins. Bred in the purple by Sigun Carlson, out of an imported bitch, Int.

Int. and Nord. Ch. Sternroc Ginza and her daughter, Int. and Nord. Ch. Ginzan's Madame Butterfly.

and Nord.. Ch. Sternroc Ginza by Int.and Nord. Ch. Riu Gu Bampei, and owned by Eva Bjarlund, he gained his Swedish title at ten months of age. He had to wait until he was over a year old for his Nordic title as, although he had won the necessary qualifications, he was too young to take the award.

I have to admit a very personal interest in Yammie, as he was called. I judged him in Sweden and was so taken with him that I asked Miss Bjarlund if she would consider sending him to England to let me show him. She gave it quite a lot of thought and then said: "We will come and sleep in your hotel room tonight. Only if Yammie jumps on your bed to sleep can he come to England." To cut a long story short, Yammie slept on my bed

Nord. Ch. Ginzan's Butterfly Buddha.

Sw. Ch. Ginzan's Powder Puff.

and, in due course, came to England. As I co-owned a quarantine kennel there was no problem. He spent his six months in the kennel, and I was able to play with him and talk to him daily. He was solely handled by me when he was in England and easily gained his English Championship, the only Swedish-bred Jap to do so. During his stay he won lots of admirers. While he was with me, he sired one or two litters – one of his progeny went to New Zealand and became a Champion. In due course, Yammie went back to Sweden, and although not mated to many bitches there, he had an impact on the breed. He was Chin of the Year in Sweden in 1979 and 1980. His daughter, Sw. Ch. Ginzan's Yammie Princess, lived until she was 17 years of age. Her litter sister, Princess Pam, lived to the age of 14. Yammie gained multiple Group placings in Sweden, as did his sister, Int. and Nord. Ch. Ginzan's Queen Of Night, to whom Gilbert Khan gave Group 2. Their dam, Int. and Nord. Ch. Sternroc

Ginza, was also placed in Groups. Yammie was born on June 25th 1977 and lived for nearly 14 years.

The Ginzan's kennel of Sigun Carlson has continued breeding and showing successful dogs, including: Int. and Nord. Ch. Ginzan's Butterfly Lion, owned by Ulla Bergstrom (Snoklippans Kennel) who, during his 15 years, made a great impact on the breed and sired 13 Champion children; Int. Ch. Ginzan's Buddha Builder, top Chin in the 1980s in Denmark and West Germany; Danish Ch. Ginzan's Crown Prince, a Yamadori son; and Ch. Ginzan's Be A Honey, who also made a great impression in Denmark. Currently Sw. Ch. Ginzan's Powder Puff and his Swedish Champion litter sister Ginzan's Buff Beauty – both red and whites – are keeping up the traditions of this outstanding kennel.

A well-known Champion of the 1980s, Int. and Nor. Ch. Lyckodrommens Wakate, was the top winning Chin in 1980-81, including BOB at the Swedish

Swedish Obedience Ch. Borgtuna's Gim.

Japanese Chin National Speciality, bred by Ulla Wessberg/Karlberg, and owned by Monica and Leif Burnas. The Linbacken kennels of Barbro Ericson (now Stensson) have had their share of success, one of their best-known dogs being S. and N. Ch. Linbackens Spader Ess, sired by Yamadori.

I have a letter, written in 1978, from May Robertshaw (of the internationally-known Lotusgrange prefix for Pekingese and Japanese Chins), telling me about her judging at the Stockholm International Show. A dog in the Youth Class really took her eye – his name was just Pondus – who won his class, took the CAC and Best of Breed. He was too young to qualify for the CACIB. She then found out it was his very first show, and the first show for his owner too. As she said, it must have been an exhibitor's dream come true when he went on to win a very strong Toy Group under the well-known American judge Edd Bivin. It just goes to show that you do not have to be a well-

known face to get to the top!

Cecilia Holmstedt is the only Swedish all-round judge to have bred Japanese Chins. She had two litters under her Ceholms prefix, then went into Japanese Spitz.

Pekka Jappinen, originally from Finland, has lived in Sweden for many years, with the Fuinrando Kennels of Japanese Chins and Cornish Rex cats. He has been active in Chins since the early 1970s. In the 1980s, he imported from the Jadel kennels in the USA, bringing in Int. Ch. Jadel's Mikado No Sunking Taro and later importing a lemon and white Am. and Can. Champion, Jadel's Jotaru. Other American imports include Int. Am. Mex. and SF Ch. (Hungarian Winner '82) Jadel's Chuji, and Tosaho Reason To Be Cheerful, now nine years old and a successful stud dog occasionally shown in Veteran classes.

Am. Nord. Dk. Ch. des Nantes 1986 Tommi-Sans Twink was sired by Eng. and Am. Ch. Apocodeodar Magic Dragon,

153

Fuinrando Asai.

who was exported to the USA when his owners, the Stevensons, emigrated from Scotland to Australia.

Pekka did not only import from America and Europe. Am. NZ and Nord. Ch. Kyasha Shimogamo, bred by Mary Newton of New Zealand, joined his kennel some time ago. He is well known for exhibiting all over Europe – and the rest of the world!

Pekka is in the fortunate position of being able to exhibit at the World Shows, and has made up World Winners in various categories. Int. S and N Ch. NW 91 Fuinrando Asai, born in December 1988, by Int. Multi. Ch. Tommi-Sans Twink-Ling ex Int. S and N Ch. Fuinrando Teller, was BOB at the Japan Kennel Club exhibition under Mr Uryu of Japan. Asai has been the Number 1 Chin in Sweden, and was also BOB at the World Show in Brussels.

Into the 1990s, Pekka is still making his mark. Two of his latest stars in the team are S. Ch. SV 93 Fuinrando Yo George, who was World Junior Winner in 1994 and European Winner in 1995 with many wins to his credit, and Fuinrando Cinq Rideaux VRF and Arg. WW '93, after

competing in the World Show held in Argentina in 1993.

Throughout the years, other kennels of note that will be found behind many of today's pedigrees are: the Garms kennel of Margit Jansson which bred the top winning bitch in 1983, Sw. Ch. Garms Isadora; the Goat Wool kennels of M. Ekstrom; Petterson's Linroos line; Akerholmens of Iris Gustavsson; Hammarangens of Ingrid Carlsson; Linroos of Gun-Britt Petersson; and Lyckodrommens of Ulla Wessberg (now Karlberg).

Although interest in the breed has diminished in recent years, it is good to know there are new fanciers starting to show and import. Among these are Ethos (A. Edin); Kitteka (Kristina Lundell); and, relatively new in the 1990s, Jappegardens (Inga Lill Orremark) and June Hallerberg's Penny Lane Kennels. It looks as if there will be a future for the Japanese Chin in Sweden.

FRANCE
Like many European countries, France does not have a Japanese Chin Club. Chins are catered for by the Club du

Pékinois et du Japonais, and often team up with King Charles Spaniels and Cavalier King Charles Spaniels when shows are held, although each breed is judged individually.

STUD BOOK RECORDS
The first Chin recorded in the French Stud Book was a bitch 'Amida' owned by Mme Ida Cohen of Paris in 1901. Sadly, there is no information of origin.

For a period of 50 years from 1901 to 1958, no statistics are available. Although there were ten registrations for the breed in 1958, numbers dwindled, and only one or two a year were registered until 1972, when there were 11. In 1975 it went up to 18, and really seemed to take off in 1976 with 58. However, registrations were up and down for the next few years reaching a further high of 84 in 1988. The popularity of the breed jumped to 197 registrations in 1994.

CLUB RE-FORMED
In 1966/67, Mme S.H. Delauney (whose affix is Vivier Du Cour) reformed Le Club du Pékinois et du Japonais. During the next few years some small kennels appeared – and disappeared – until 1973/4, when Michele Le Royer's kennel, Valecourt Des Grés Valois, came to the fore. She worked very hard for the promotion of the breed in France, and made many visits to British Championship Shows just to study the breed. Her kennel gained more and more respect and she made up a number of Champions, always with the improvement of the breed at heart. She became president of the Club du Pékinois et du Japonais. To increase the gene pool in her kennel, she imported several Sternroc dogs, among them

Sternroc Kashi and Sternroc Kai. Both became International Champions and Kashi was placed 3rd in the 9th Group (Toy Group) at Poitiers International Show in 1981. Mme Le Royer was a very keen and dedicated breeder/exhibitor until family circumstances made it impossible for her to continue. Current president of the club is Mme Fages. Suzanne Dereu has also been closely connected with the club over a number of years.

PROMINENT KENNELS
The Wang-Fu affix of Mme Wira-Mazoyer is a household name within the breed in Europe, as she has made up more than seven Int. Chs., and several more gained their French titles.

Mme Nazaret of Fontaine A L'Hermite kennels is a relative newcomer to the breed, as she obtained her first Chin in 1991. She based her breeding on Wang Fu lines and made up two Int. Chs., F'shinsucke De Wang Fu and Hidenka De Wang Fu, who was also a winner at the European Show in Dortmund in 1993. Mme Nazaret breeds one or two litters a year and has a permanent kennel of about eight dogs, only adding puppies she keeps from her breeding. Fuinrando Ibsen, Lux. Ch. 1995, and Fuinrando Danuta De Nazaret are recent additions.

Mme Wasserman-Braga's Lutins Fu Pai Chins number ten or more Champions, with at least half homebred. She imported Amantra Don Juro, who now holds a French title.

Mme Wertbrouck-Nau has a couple of English imports in her Manoir De Kergreen kennels – Finchfield Shinshi Of Homerbrent, who became a French Champion, and Navron Bozu, who

LEFT: Ch. Fiery Samourai du Terikomi.

BELOW LEFT: Fuinrando Ibsen.

BELOW RIGHT: Ch. Furioso du Terikomi.

gained both French and Int. titles. These two have given her new bloodlines to add to those of her existing homebred Champions.

Swedish and English breeding feature in the background of the Terikomi kennels of Hélène Marcinkowski. Int. Ch. Ib Don Juan Du Midnight Sun goes back to Sternroc Mikki on his sire's side, and his dam is Ulvus Yashodara, who is Swedish and goes back to Lotusgrange and Yevot breeding. Ch. Fiery Samourai Du Terikomi, sired by Mme Marcinkowski's Don Juan out of Dunloo Desi Yamabuki, bred by the UK's Mrs A. Dilley, has a full brother, Ch. Furioso Du Terikomi.

Mme Marcinkowski's dogs have competed very successfully in Agility competitions and Don Juan, Fiery Samourai and Fortunio Du Terikomi have done extraordinarily well, becoming French Agility Champions and competing in the Finale Pedigree Pal Chambord. While a number of Chins do compete in Obedience in various countries, these are the first known in Agility competition. This type of competition, as Mme Marcinkowski says, "needs a good chest, a good heart, good health, good constitution and a good mind." Apart from French and Agility champions, her kennel houses Fr. Nord. Ch. Fuinrando Kerim.

The Du Midnight Sun kennels of Ann-Christin Peupion contained three lovely champions all being exhibited at the same time: Int. and Nord. Ch. Ali Du Midnight Sun; Fr. and Int. Ch. Cho Cho Du Midnight Sun; and Int. S. SF. and F. Ch. Snoklippans Su-Zu-Ki, the latter from Ulla Bergstrom's breeding in Sweden. These are just a few of the many Champions of Mme Peupion.

Fr. Ch. Romain De Valecourt Des Grés Valois and Fuinrando Tai Sho are a couple of French Champions housed in Mme Salvini's Grosse Roche kennels, other than her own illustrious homebred Champions.

Mme Folliard is a successful breeder of Yorkshire Terriers as well as Japanese Chins, and the Chin she bred, Jenji-San Of The Wreath Royal, was a World Youth Winner at Brussels 1995. She also owns his sire Hito Samourai – a French Champion at 15 months.

As can be seen there is a good nucleus of breeders keeping interest in Chins alive in France.

GERMANY

The German book, *Der Vornehme Zimmerhund,* written about Pekingese, King Charles Spaniels and Japanese Chins, and printed in 1929, gives the history of the breed in Germany as follows:

"In 1881 Baroness Ulm-Erbach received a couple of Chins from her brother. More followed and she became the first enthusiastic Chin breeder. In the 1890s a few Chins were exhibited at dog shows and, in spite of the fact that there were few good specimens, they were much admired and people quickly became interested in the breed. Some of these people eventually imported dogs direct from Japan and these, together with those of Baroness Ulm-Erbach, became the foundation of the German breeding stock of Japanese Chins.

"Mrs Hagel and Mrs Meltz played an important part in the breed inasmuch as Mrs Hagel lived for some years in Japan prior to the 1914-18 War, and built her breeding on stock she acquired in Japan."

157

Pia van Hoeven, a famous singer and actress, was a breeder of Chins for more than 50 years and exhibited at most of the important European shows. She was a familiar figure in Berlin, pedalling round on her bicycle with the basket in front full of Chins. Her dogs had long and full lives, some living to over 15 years of age.

Christa Franzan purchased Alstella Josiphina from Mrs Sargant in the UK. She was best bitch in the breed at the Europa Seiger in Dortmund in 1978. More recently, Frau Franzan exported Raikon Vom Schloss Orlanda to Barbara Vallance of the Myagi Sato Japanese Chins in America. She is very thrilled with him, as he has already obtained his first Major toward his American Championship from the 6-9 month puppy class. Frau Franzan has imported a red and white bitch puppy from Barbara, Miyagi's Sure To Be Brandy.

Miss Syska owned Lewisia Sarita, purchased from Mrs Reeves (the mother of Mrs Sargant), and Sarita won the Youth Bitch award in the breed at the World Show in Innsbruck.

Max Kaatz, owner of the Haus Sonnenschein kennels in Nettetal, near Düsseldorf, not only exported dogs to the USA, but his stock was well-known all over Europe, where they won many prestigious events. Mi-Chu vom Haus Sonnenschein was a winner at the two-day show in Berlin. Ut-Chu vom Haus Sonnenschein went to Ursula Hill of Philadelphia, which was rather a full circle for Mrs Hill, who was born near Berlin, emigrated to Newfoundland after the Second World War, and then went on to live in Philadelphia. It was not until she went to visit her brother in the 1970s that she saw her first Jap, one of several out for a walk with a woman. This turned out to be Pia van Hoeven. Ursula fell in love with Chins, and she and Pia became good friends. About a year later, Ursula's brother went to visit her in the USA and took Shen-Chou vom Haus Sonnenschein with him. Shen-Chou was not a happy show dog, but did win BOW at the Westminster Show in New York. Ut-Chu was a born show dog and gained his American championship with Group placings

Another prominent breeder of Japanese Chins, Mrs Wernicke from the Berlin area, sadly died of a heart attack while out walking her dogs.

Hanny Steinmetz was a well-known breeder/exhibitor for many years but is, I believe, no longer active.

The German Chin Club (which is under the umbrella of the Internationaler Club Für Japan-Chin, Peking-Palasthunde und Toy Spaniel) had a breed stand at the Dortmund Sieger show this year.

AUSTRIA
The Stud Book records of the Austrian Kennel Club for Japanese Chins only go back as far as 1946, the end of World War Two, during which earlier records were destroyed.

The Achbach-Klause kennel of Therese Lechner was at the forefront of the breed from 1948 to about 1968, usually breeding one or two litters a year. Between 1946 and August 1994, there were 129 Japs registered in Austria.

The top winning Chin must have been Japanese-bred Kayanokiso Fumi, a black and white bitch, bred by Yonkeo Watanabe and owned by Trude Bauer, who piloted her through her illustrious career. She won a CACIB in Japan, eight in Europe, was a Sieger winner in Salzburg and Innsbruck making her an Austrian and International Champion, and she became a World Champion at the World Show in Verona in 1980.

Other successful Austrian breeders in the early days were the Eibesbrunn kennels of Franz Granzl; Frieda Capek's Capekgarten kennels; Mia Winklmann's well-known Donaustrand prefix; the Barockschlossel kennels of Maria Wolf; and Grete Reinisch's Yokonsya line. More recently, Marta Edelmannova, Lenka Praskova and Jana Gatakova have developed an interest in the breed.

Ch. Kamp Keizan van Senzaai-Shu.

HOLLAND

Holland is a country famous for cheese, windmills, tulips and, perhaps not quite so well-known, dog-lovers. While the most popular breeds are Bouvier des Flandres, German Shepherds and Golden Retrievers, there is still a devoted band of Japanese Chin enthusiasts.

The Japanese Chin does not have its own breed club in the Netherlands, but is incorporated under the umbrella of the "Pekingese en Dwergspanielclub". On April 16th 1899, records from De Raad van Beheer op Kynologisch Gebied in Nederland – otherwise known as the Dutch Kennel Club – show that there was a Japanese Chin exhibited at the Amsterdam show by the name of "Chisay, whelped March 25th 1898, owned by J. Jomelli".

In 1907, a Chin from Belgium was registered in Holland and the breeder was a Mr Hong Hi Hang, which leads one to believe it could have been imported from the Orient! The next registration is in 1917 when Togo was listed as owned by

Int. Ch. Crossgate Xultan.

H. Habert of Amsterdam. Other records were lost during the war. A very early breeder, Mrs A. van de Berg-Voigt, created a lot of interest at dog shows with her male Chin, Ch. Manchukuo, who was imported from England. We have a stud book number for him but no further details.

In the 1930s Mr T. van Laarschot had a well-known kennel of Chins, the Van Walcheren kennel. His last dogs died at the end of World War Two because, at that time, there were no vaccines available

W.M. Bleeker-Jansen and her dogs.

to combat distemper, etc. The first litter was born, and registered in the Dutch Stud Book, in 1934. The breeder, Francien van Douwe-Moerkoert, is really the pioneer of the breed in Holland. Her kennel is Van Akita. There were three puppies in her first litter, by Jumjap out of Sunneke Van Hittepetit. Mrs van Douwe became friendly with Mrs Craufurd and Miss Sully in England, and visited them several times, purchasing dogs from them, and from Miss Tovey. Among these imports were Homerbrent Oishi Of Yevot, Prince Shogun Of Camplane, and Mussme Of Riu Gu.

In 1969, Magret Steinmeijer-Wagner inadvertently came into the breed. I say inadvertently because she went to visit an acquaintance in Germany where she saw a little Japanese Chin sitting in the snow in an outside kennel trying to defend herself from a German Shepherd. She felt so sorry for her, she bought the bitch and took her back to Holland. Her name was Shu-Tai vom Haus Sonnenschein, whelped in May 1967, sired by a Japanese import, Hana No Kamakura Mikasa, out of Quicki vom Haus Sonnenschein. In due course, Magret decided she would like to breed from her. After a lot of enquiries, she was put in touch with Francien van Douwe and phoned. During the course of the conversation, Magret asked Francien how many Japanese Chins she had and was surprised to be told: "It may seem strange to you but I don't know precisely. I think somewhere between 46 and 49." She went to visit, they counted, and there were 46.

The choice of stud dog was also decided

in a somewhat novel manner. Magret says: "On the appointed day when Shu-Tai went to be mated, Francien van Douwe opened the door to the room of the 'willing studs' and those who wanted to breed came out. The owner of the bitch did not make the decision, the male made it for her. The willing dog came out from under the cupboard. His name was Mon Choux Van Akita. This sounds a never-to-be-forgotten experience!

In due course, the bitch whelped four puppies and there was no turning back for Magret Steinmeijer then. She kept one out of the litter, started going to shows and has been breeding and showing ever since. In 1976, she decided it was time to introduce some new blood and went to the UK, where she purchased Crossgate Xultan from Peggy Searl. This dog had a phenomenal show career, becoming a national and International Champion, Luxembourg Champion and, in 1981 at the World Show in Dortmund, he won BOB and became World Champion over an entry of 46 Chins.

Mrs Bleeker-Jansen is another well-known name in the breed in Holland. She had Chins in 1940 when she lived in the former Dutch East Indies. On her return, she kept only males and had 16. She was not a breeder, but her dogs were used at stud.

Mrs T.J. Slooten owned Navron Omi, purchased from the Smiths in UK and sired by their Japanese import. Omi became an International Champion and World Champion in 1986.

Mrs P. Heerkens Verschuren was well-known in several Toy breeds some years ago. She bred Ch. Chi-Qui v.d. Heerschuur, who became such a famous winner for the vom Paenbruch kennel in

Switzerland.

In 1993, only 41 puppies were registered in Holland.

SWITZERLAND

Without a doubt, the most outstanding winner in the breed came from the Zwinger von Paenbruch kennels of Dieter Deppenmeier and his partner Walter Holtorf, based in Zurich. Their winners featured both red and white and black and white dogs.

Their red and white homebred Int. and Swiss Chs. of the 1970s and '80s – Eishi and Geisha vom Paenbruch – were sired by Swiss Ch. Addislea Yoshono. Yoshono was bred by Ann Francis (UK), won his Swiss and German titles and also won a Toy Group in Switzerland. Among their black and white winners were Int. Chs. Bishonen and Boya vom Paenbruch, both sired by the English import Crossgate Xultan.

However, their most famous Japanese Chin was the bitch Ch. Chi-Qui v.d. Heerschuur, bred by Mrs P. Heerkens Verschuren of the Netherlands. She was Int. Swiss, Austrian, Italian, French, German, Dutch and Belgian Champion, winning top shows in three countries and spanning a four-year period. She won BOB at the famous Amsterdam Winners Show three times. Chi-Qui was their foundation bitch and produced many winning children and grandchildren.

A great achievement for any Japanese Chin kennel is to win a Breeders Group at an International show. Dieter did this twice with a team of four at Bern in 1980, and in 1983 with a team of six at Zurich International – the Jubilee Show celebrating 100 years of the SKC.

AUSTRALIA
SOUTH AUSTRALIA

In the early 1920s, Mrs A. Williams 'Rosalea' of Goodwood, S. Australia, was regularly exhibiting Japanese Spaniels. At the same time, she was also the leading lady in Pomeranians in that State. From two catalogues dated 1918 and 1919 for the 8th and 9th Grand Shows of the Collie, Pomeranian and Pekingese Club of SA (incorporating Toy dogs and cats, a club that is now the Colomeke Club of SA), we know that Mrs Williams exhibited a pair of Japanese Spaniels at each of these shows. These were her two foundation dogs, Rosalea Countess Ito (Sire: Fu Fu, imp. Dam, Krinsio; whelped 8th September 1917; breeder Mrs Whitehouse). Here the trail ends.

There was a revival in the breed in the mid 1970s, when Ron and Margaret Wood imported from Koto-Chin (NZ) and also bought from Merv Burgman's Inverglen line (Victoria), and Keith and Lillias Radford established their Eradan kennel.

Donna Skoda purchased Interstar Jimmu – sired by Ranella Johnny out of Koto-Chin Ruini – from the Rubeden kennels. Jimmu was actually bred by

Aust. Ch. Chinigan Lil Teddy Bear.

Helen and John Bowgen (NSW), and he became a top winner and sired a number of Champions. At this time, Donna's prefix was Sukuranbo, which was changed to Chinigan in 1985.

Undoubtedly the most successful kennel in the State today must be Chinsan, owned by Jenny and Geoff Caird, a dedicated, single-minded couple, who knew exactly what they wanted and have been very successful in achieving it. Their stock is in demand throughout the whole of Australasia. The foundation of this kennel goes back to eight imports

Pictured left to right: Aust. Ch. Chinsan Saishi, Aust. Ch. Koto-Chin Masataka and Aust. NZ Ch. Koto-Chin Tobiyashi.

purchased from the Koto-Chin kennels of Mrs Marbeck in New Zealand, and the Cairds have successfully followed this breeding ever since.

Chinsans have won BIS at all but one of the Japanese Chin Club Shows, and breed expert Dr Dennis Maher, who judged the Club Championship Show in 1995, awarded Ch. Chinsan Kikoshi (black and white) Best in Show, and his sire, Ch. Chinsan Tama, runner up. Kikoshi is now owned and exhibited by Shane Buzza who, in turn, has founded his line on the Chinsans. The Cairds have recently exported stock back to Mrs Marbeck and also sent some to W. Australia. Their success is not only due to careful line-breeding, but incorporates good feeding and a natural life for their dogs who enjoy running in the country. They also have to know a lot about potential owners before they will let them have a puppy!

The Rubeden prefix, owned by Brown and Tassie, has been very prominent in this State. They purchased Ranella Johnny, the UK import, from Helen Bowgen in the early 1980s. Sadly, ill health forced this successful partnership to retire from breeding and showing a few years ago.

QUEENSLAND

Jenny Claydon was one of the early importers from New Zealand, when she brought in Taeko Of Rosemarie in 1967. She recalls she was often disillusioned when exhibiting this dog. The breed was few and far between in those days, and many judges had never seen a Japanese Chin. There was little reading matter on the breed other than the Breed Standard, which some judges took time to read but others did not. In spite of this, Taeko

became a Champion later that same year. A few months elapsed and another import, Tasha Of Rosemarie, was purchased from the same NZ kennel. Tasha and Taeko were mated and a litter of six puppies resulted. Tasha gained his Australian title, and this was the start of Miss Claydon's Mingdon kennel. This kennel has the distinction of showing the first Chin in the State of Queensland, and was the first to win a Challenge at the Brisbane Royal Show. Tasha was eventually sold to Joan Fieldhouse, who bred a litter sired by him in December 1967 and, in turn, these puppies became the foundation of the Invergowrie Chins.

Violet Howe owned her first Chin in 1942 in the UK, started breeding them and has been 'hooked' ever since. She was closely associated with the late Miss Tovey of Yevot fame. Miss Howe took her Chinchivi prefix to Australia when she emigrated in 1974, and has continued successfully breeding Chins and Chihuahuas ever since. Ch. Chinchivi Kiski CD, bred by Miss Howe and owned by Pam Large, is the only Chin in Australia to have his CD title. In December 1983, Miss Howe imported Dunloo Desu Koebi from Mrs Dilley (UK) and he became an Australian Champion. Chinchivi Suki Too was exported to the USA. Miss Howe is a popular judge in Australia.

Dee Byster of the Mikadochin prefix has been in Chins since 1988, and has been very successful winning Challenges and BOBs at many of the Royal Shows. Among the outstanding successes were Ch. Elharad Bimyo, who won the Group at the Northern Classic at eight months of age. At the Gold Coast Canine Club in 1991 Mikadochins took both dog and bitch Challenges, Reserve Dog Challenge and Champion Puppy of Group. They have done a repeat mating of their all-Champion litter, and new 'baby' Mikadochin Ieyasu is already making a name for himself.

Yebbli kennels, owned by Brian and Barbara Bielby, have been making up Champions in the breed since the early 80s, and feature both black and white and red and white Australian champions, with red and white Ch. Seiko Silver Sameai holding a NZ title as well.

VICTORIA
In 1974, Merv Burgmann visited New Zealand and was so captivated by the Chins he saw there that he purchased a bitch, Tomomi Of Koto-Chin, followed by a dog and two more bitches the following year. Thus were the Inverglen kennels formed. He did well with his stock, winning Reserve Challenges at both Melbourne and Sydney Royals with Aus. Ch. Kunshu Of Koto-Chin, who was the first Chin to win Best in Group in Victoria from the puppy class. Kunshu was eventually acquired by Pat Douglas from Western Australia. Between 1976 and 1979 he bred six litters from three bitches. Sadly, Mr Burgmann has now deserted Japanese Chins for Cavalier King Charles Spaniels.

In 1976, Mrs M. Fullerton purchased a bitch from the Inverglen line who proved to be the foundation of her Fuchon breeding. Inverglen Monoko was BOB at Melbourne Royal in 1980. Imports from New Zealand joined the Fuchon kennels, and several Champions were made up. Mrs Fullerton is still active in the breed.

Since the late 1980s, Shane Buzza has been the most prominent exhibitor in Victoria with his Buzzalong kennels, based on Chinsan lines. He has had outstanding success in winning Group and BIS awards, notably with Ch. Chinsan Bessei and Ch. Chinsan Masanori, who was bred by the Cairds and handled by Shane to win BIS at the 1989 Toy Dog Club of Victoria's Championship Show. It is interesting to note that all of these go back to one of the original dogs or bitches imported by the Cairds – a classic example of how careful breeding can pay off.

There was a decline in fanciers of the breed in the early 1980s, as both the 1981 and 1983 Melbourne Royals attracted only four exhibits. More people in Victoria became interested later in the decade and breeding and showing numbers increased, so that, in 1994, 35 Chins were entered in the Melbourne Royal and 30 in 1995. From this, it would appear that the breed now has a good hold in Victoria.

NEW SOUTH WALES
Probably the most universally known name in Australian Chins is that of Dr Dennis Maher. No record of the breed in this country would be complete without full mention of him. His interest in the breed goes back to before 1970. He purchased his first Chin from Joy Marbeck (Koto-Chin NZ), originally intending to have just one bitch. However, there were two bitches in the litter and he bought both of them, then registered his affix, Samedi. He handled Hokkaido Prince Toshi (the progeny of the two Camplane imports) for Mrs Harrison. Toshi gained his Australian title and was sold to Mrs Marbeck. Toshi's dam Cho Cho then went to live with

Aust. Ch. Tieebah Hy Oko.

Dennis for the rest of her life.

This led Dennis to correspond with Miss Sully (the UK breeder of Cho Cho). When her dear friend Mrs Craufurd of the Riu Gu's died, Miss Sully was asked if she wanted any of the Riu Gu puppies. So, Riu Gu Bimyo flew to Australia. He had a great career, making history in the process. When he was released from Perth quarantine station, he went to his first show where he won Best Puppy in the Toy Group, at an all-breed Championship show, and never looked back! He was the first Chin to win Best In Show at an all-breed Championship Show when he won this award at Liverpool and District Championship Show over 1671 entries (269 Toys). He notched up another BIS award at an all-breed Championship show and two Res. BIS awards, as well as picking up many Challenges on the way.

Dr Maher, as he was by then, accepted a position in Japan and Bimyo went to Mary Fitz-Patrick Netz in Hawaii, later moving to the mainland with her. He was to gain three titles during his life:

Australian, New Zealand and American Champion. Dennis spent 12 years in Japan, and visited a number of dog shows. Japanese Chins were shown in the Japanese Breeds Group. His observations on the breed there, at that time, were that: "the Japanese have a size problem with their big ones, but their small ones are really small and fine-boned, with hair dripping off them."

On his return to Australia, he was very pleased with the improvement in quality during his absence. At the Chin Club Championship Show in Victoria in July 1995, there were 72 Chins and it was here that he made Ch. Chinsan Kikoshi BIS.

Mrs M. Eather established Tieebah kennels in the late 1970s, and was primarily breeding Lhasa Apsos at that time. She purchased her first Chin in 1980 and, from the result of a mating between Yevot Shotoko (imported by Miss Howe) and Ch. Rurigakirei Oko in 1987, achieved her first real taste of success in the breed with Ch. Tieebah Hy Oko, who has been the recipient of many Challenges, BOBs and Group wins. His offspring, Chs. Tieebah Oshaku and Niji, have been following in father's footsetps with many good wins.

The Welona affix of Miss Graham was based on Tieebah and Chinsan breeding, and her Ch. Tieebah Nikko was a well-known winner.

Julie Fluerty's Aus. and NZ Ch. Seiko Shintgo Edo (imp. NZ) was BIS at Newcastle Merewether all-breed Championship Show in 1994. Her lines are based on the Seiko kennel in NZ.

The Interstar kennels of John and Helen Bowgen purchased Cassilove Smart Alec from Mrs Proudford, who imported

him from the UK in 1976. He was a dog who attained his Australian title with ease. The Bowgens, of course, were tied up with Donna Skoda, as can be seen under the South Australia section.

Other prominent Chins owned by exhibitors in this State include Mrs Dewhurst's Ch. Thankdew Kimi Sumo, Christine Holm's Ch. Tannashar Lord Falkor, and Mrs Pulton's Ch. Tieebah Rika. Mrs Kingdom has enjoyed a very successful run with Ch. Sharonde Sachiko, as have Mrs and Miss Silver with Shintoo Nikawei. In 1983/4, Ron Uren's Windswept Chins were a force to be reckoned with, but he has not been active of late.

WESTERN AUSTRALIA
The first Japanese Chin to make an appearance in the show ring in Western Australia was Aus. Ch. Kunshu Of Koto-Chin, bred by Joy Marbeck in New Zealand and exported to Merv Burgmann of the Inverglen line – and it was he who piloted the dog to his title in Victoria. Pat Douglas acquired Kunshu who, during his show career, notched up several Group wins.

In 1978 and 1979, Mrs Douglas purchased Inverglen Kosho and Inverglen Michiyo, daughters of Riu Gu Bimyo, to be joined by Inverglen Kentaro. These formed the foundation stock of most Western Australian Chins. Ch. Leng Dayana San, a red and white, was the first WA-bred Chin to gain her Championship. She was bred from Kentaro and Michiyo.

Pat Douglas and Irene Birkett went into partnership under the Leng prefix, breeding Japanese Chins and Shih Tzus. However, after five years, the partnership dissolved. Mrs Birkett continued with the

Aust. Ch. Chinleng Topsi San: The first Japanese Chin to win BIS at an all-breed Ch. Show in Western Australia.

prefix, breeding Shih Tzus, while Mrs Douglas adopted the Chinleng prefix and concentrated on breeding Chins. Shortly after this, she purchased Koto-Chin Osamu from Joy Marbeck. He was a son of NZ Ch. Sternroc Yam Sekai Ichi, in turn the son of a Swedish dog who gained his UK and Nordic titles, Ginzans Prince Yamadori Of Sternroc. From a mating of Osamu and Michiyo, Pat Douglas bred Ch. Chinleng Topsi San, who had the distinction of being the first Chin in Western Australia to win BIS at the WA Kennel Club Show (an all-breed championship Show) in May 1988, only the second of the breed to achieve this honour in either Australia or New Zealand. She continued her winning ways with Res. BIS at other WA Toy Dog Specialist Club Championship and Open Shows, and was Best Veteran at one of these shows in 1993, which was her last appearance in the show ring. Pat Douglas has now transferred her Chinleng prefix to Brenda Fordham of the Aventura Kennels, but continues to take an active interest in the breed, always striving for improvement.

The decade 1980-1990 brought an increase in the number of Chin exhibitors in this State. They were joined by breed enthusiasts who moved to WA from other parts of the country. However, many of these owners did not continue in the breed for one reason or another. Only recently has there has been an upsurge. Three Chinsan dogs from Jenny Caird in South Australia have arrived and gained their titles, and now there are several very keen exhibitors.

ACT
Betty Kingdom, of the Sharonde affix, and Dorothy and daughter Natalie Silver, with the Siatori Chins, are active breeders in this State.

TASMANIA
There is just one breeder currently active here, Joan Pettit of the Wisawai kennel, which also houses Chihuahuas.

SUMMARY
From this history it can be seen that the stock in Australia and New Zealand is very closely inter-related, and Britain has played its part in their breeding programmes. There is plenty of interest in Japanese Chins in this part of the world, and a great deal of enthusiasm. One can only hope that as travel grows easier and less expensive, and with the hoped for

demise of quarantine, we will all one day have the pleasure of exhibiting our dogs at the same shows, and making plans to preserve type and improve our lovely breed.

NEW ZEALAND
FIRST CHINS IN NEW ZEALAND

In about 1960, Bishop and Mrs Baines emigrated from England to Wellington, New Zealand. The newly-appointed Anglican Bishop and his wife brought with them a Japanese Chin, Uso Of Riu Gu. They decided he needed a companion, and wrote to Mrs Craufurd who eventually sent them Neisan Of Forsedene. Neisan arrived about two years after the Baineses had landed, and came by ship.

Uso Of Riu Gu, a black and white dog
Sire: Atlatus Of Riu Gu
Dam: Robwood Chin Rubellite Of Riu Gu
Neisan Of Forsedene, a black and white bitch

(note: this affix not to be confused with Gorsedene)

Sire: Eng. Ch. Mosaru Of Yevot
Dam: Megan Of Margaretha.

These two Chins produced the first litter of Japanese Chins recorded at the New Zealand Kennel Club. The litter was born on 16th December 1963, and consisted of three dogs and two bitches. This was the foundation of the Baines' Sojoin Kennels. One of the bitches, Kiki Of Sojoin, became a Champion and was owned by Eve O'Connor who founded the Rosemarie kennels

The second recorded litter was a repeat of the first mating, and three bitches and one dog were whelped on the 11th March 1965. From this litter Mrs O'Connor took the bitch Sojoin Matsuko.

NEW IMPORTS

Eve O'Connor then imported Tassha Of Riu Gu from Western Australia. Tassha had been imported into Australia by some English immigrants. The family flew out to their new home, but their dogs were sent by cargo ship. Tassha, unfortunately, was the only one to survive the journey. He was sired by Qu's Masterpiece Of Riu Gu and his dam was Aronia Of Riu Gu.

Tassha and Kiki were mated, and produced the third recorded litter in New Zealand, whelped on the 21st August 1965. This union only produced one bitch, later Ch. My Minya Of Rosemarie. This bitch, in her first litter, whelped on the 14th December 1966, produced the first red and white Chin registered in NZ – Hushimoto Of Rosemarie.

All three English imports were the mainstays of breeding stock until Eve O'Connor again imported from England Yancha Of Riu Gu (later NZ Ch., born

James, son of the Rt. Rev. H.W. Baines, Bishop of Wellington, on the lawn at Bishopcourt with the first family of Japanese Chin to be born in New Zealand.

on the 3rd July 1967).

Sire: Eng. Ch. Nyorai Of Riu Gu
Dam: Taki San Of Riu Gu

Yancha was used extensively at stud. Shortly after this, Mrs O'Connor was unable to continue breeding and, in 1970, Yancha moved to the Koto-Chin kennels of Joy Marbeck. Joy had already purchased a bitch, Monoko Of Rosemarie, from Mrs O'Connor. These two breeders were very conscientious, and it was from their stock that many of the top winning NZ and Australian Chins were bred.

In a letter to the author in 1981 Mrs Marbeck wrote: "After receiving Yancha from my friend Eve, I bred a number of puppies from him and kept two of his sons, who later gave me puppies that I preferred to those from Yancha himself. Among these was Mikado Of Rosemarie (bred by Mrs O'Connor), and between him and his sire and several good bitches I carried out two separate line breeding programmes, the end result being two superb little bitches, Ch. Toshiko Of Koto-Chin and Ch. Toshiba Of Koto-Chin. As far as my breeding went, there was no 'inbreeding' forced on to me."

In the early 1970s, the two Camplane imports produced two dog puppies. Hokaido Prince Toshi was purchased by Mrs Marbeck from Mrs Harrison, and his brother Shiki was sold as a pet and never used for breeding. At this time, there was top class stock in New Zealand and the 70s were boom years for Japanese Chins, with approximately 20 exhibited at every show. This, unfortunately, is not the case in the mid-1990s.

Imports from the UK in the 1970s were Valevan Penitino, Carraig Kitchi-Ro Of

Aust. NZ Ch. Samedi Tatsuaki.

Sternroc and Addislea Anuska Of Valevan. Riu Gu Bimyo, who was imported into Australia from the UK by Dennis Maher, was exported to Joy Marbeck (after attaining his NZ title he returned to Australia). Samedi Higashi Miya was another exported from Australia, bred by Dennis Maher, who also exported Aust. and NZ Ch. Samedi Miho – the latter two dogs going to Mary Newton of the Shimogamo kennels.

BREEDERS AND THEIR AFFIXES
Active breeder/exhibitors in the 1970s were:

Koto-Chin	Joy Marbeck
Kamavero	Verna Ingley
Glengordon	Val Ormandy

Mikado	Hannah McHardy
Seiko	Val Clarke-Benson
Cherrylea	Dolly Christie
Kino	Val Garvey and
	Cathy Garvey-Webb
Chinsai	Loraine Christianson
Durylyn	Fay and Charlie
	Anthony
Shimogamo	Mary Newton
Meiko	Bill Meyrick
Takada	Mrs L. Marris

Of these, only Cathy Garvey-Webb is still breeding/exhibiting, although Joy Marbeck – now an octogenarian – retains an interest in the breed, and is helping new breeder/exhibitors, the Hopes of Murasaki kennels.

In the 1970s, Mary Newton and Joy Marbeck were both breeding Chins in Auckland and exported a number of dogs to Australia, where they formed the basis of today's breeding.

Mary Newton exported a black and white dog, NZ Ch. Miki Of Shimogamo to America, where he became Am. Can. Mexican and Int. Champion. She also exported a bitch to Pekka Jappinen of Sweden, Int. and Nord.. NZ and Am. Ch. Kmyasha Shimogamo.

The Seiko kennels of Val Clarke-Benson were also very active; her stock was based on Koto-Chin. Sadly, ill health forced her to give up a couple of years ago.

TOP WINNERS

The Kino kennels of Val and Cathy Garvey-Webb were making their mark at this time on the NZ scene. NZ Ch. Akito Of Kino – one of their first Chins – made a great impact, being awarded Best Toy on several occasions and amassing a record 98 Challenges before his untimely death at the early age of three years. It must be remembered, too, that this was in the 1970s, when competition was at its hottest. His son, Koi-Inu Nama-Nari, bred and owned by Cathy Garvey-Webb, won the Baby Puppy Sweepstakes at four months of age at the NZ National in 1978, topping an entry of 135, under the illustrious and world-famous judge, the late Joe Braddon.

However, this kennel really made history when their Aust. and NZ Ch. Koto-Chin Tobiyashi, affectionately known as 'J.C.', was awarded BIS at a NZ all-breed Championship Show, the first and only one to date of his breed to achieve this. Not content with this, J.C. is also the only Chin to be dual-titled, winning BIS in two different countries. He also won Best Junior in Group at the NZ National (the best-known and most prestigious show in New Zealand) in 1989, and BIS at an all-breed Open show

Cathy Garvey-Webb with five of her Champions: Top (left to right): Ch. Kino Magin Nai Chin, Ch. Koto-Chin Mikasa, Ch. Teomoana Saki Chin, Below: Aust. NZ. Ch. Koto-Chin Tobiyashi and Ch. Kino Stit Chin Time.

in Australia. To add to his achievements, he also produced the all-Champion litter of NZ, Chs. Kino Locomochin, Kino Kwit Ya Bit Chin and the red and white Kino The Politichin. Other champion progeny include Kino Runaround Sue, Kino Dion De Mutt, Aus. Ch. Chinsan Nichiyume and Aus. Ch. Chinsan Mogwyi. Many of these are also in Group winners.

As you can see, Cathy Garvey-Webb has a good sense of fun, especially when it comes to naming her Chins. Cathy has been actively engaged in the sport of dog showing and breeding for about 25 years. It began with an Australian Terrier, but quickly spread to her all-time love, Japanese Chins, to which she has added Shih Tzus. Kino kennels is jointly owned by Cathy Garvey-Webb and her mother Val Garvey, and specialises in Toy breeds.

Hannah McHardy of Mikado kennels – again based on Koto-Chin lines – was fortunate enough to have Yancha Of Riu Gu for the last few years of his life. He produced lovely type for her, and one of his daughers, NZ Ch. Mikado Dekimono, was one of the best.

DISASTER STRIKES

The breed received a tremendous setback in the early 1980s when one of the breeders went out of Japanese Chins and, of the 35 in the kennel, all but one were put to sleep. A large amount of quality breeding stock virtually disappeared overnight, and it was a blow from which the breed in NZ has never really recovered.

PLANNED BREEDING

More imports arrived, such as Sternroc Yam Sekai Ichi (later NZ Ch.) who was

NZ Am. Can. Mex. Int. Ch. Miki of Shimogamo.

imported by Mrs Marbeck.

Sire: Ch. and Nord. Ch. Ginzan's Prince Yamadori Of Sternroc
Dam: Sternroc Sekura

This breeding actually tied in very well with earlier imports, going back to Ch. Nyorai Of Riu Gu on his sire's side. It was through Ichi, who sired NZ Ch. Koto-Chin Mikasa, mated to Mrs Marbeck's Ch. Seiko Seiera Sunset, that Jenny Caird's Aus. Ch. Koto-Chin Masataka was born. From a later litter came Cathy Garvey-Webb's BIS winner, NZ and Aus. Ch. Koto-Chin Tobiyashi.

Pictured (left to right): Ch. Koto-Chin Hideko, Koto-Chin Joyu, Ch. Koto-Chin Zeppin, Kino Evening Affair and Aust. NZ Ch. Koto-Chin Tobiyashi.

Shintoo Fuji, a red and white dog imported by Joy Marbeck from Brenda Stewart in Australia, was mated to another Australian import, Ch. Richkelarden Nasaka to produce a lovely red and white bitch, Ch Seiko Seiera Sunset. She, in turn, produced Champion stock. Her litter sister, Seiko Seiera Sunrise was retained by Val Clarke-Benson (the owner of the bitch), and was behind many of her dogs in the late 1980s. Getting back to the 1980s, imports also included Silkybeau Yen Kee from Australia, who joined Bill Meyrick's Meiko kennels before moving to the Raksha kennels, owned by Colleen Ward. It was a bitch puppy from one of this bitch's last litters, Ch. Bella Of Raksha, who joined the Kino kennels and became a very successful dam.

LATEST IMPORT

New fanciers in the breed have appeared during the 1990s. Lisa and Tony Hope, who have been in the breed for five or six years, added a Chinsan from Jenny Caird in Australia to their kennels recently, and their most recent import is Amantra Onokumi from England. This dog has half Japanese breeding.

The enthusiasm of these breeder/

exhibitors is an inspiration and there is no doubt that their dedication and thoughtful breeding programmes have paid off in terms of the good stock they have produced.

JAPAN

Prior to 1914-18, and between the two World Wars, Japanese Chins were exported to fanciers all over the world. Import registrations in various national kennel clubs bear this out. However, by the conclusion of World War Two, the breeding stock of Chins in Japan itself had been pretty well decimated.

Oudenarde Sugar Puff was sent out from England by Miss Hamilton and Mrs Tarry, to help enlarge the gene pool. He was the first Japanese Chin ever imported into Japan, and became a Champion and Asiatic Champion, producing winning stock. He went to Dr Momore who, some time later, exported a dog to the Oudenarde Kennel. This dog, Oudenarde Togo, won two Challenge Certificates in the UK. Some dogs also went from America to replenish stock in Japan.

Towards the end of the 1940s, interest was regained in the breed and five main lines were established in Japan.

172

Oudenarde Sugar Puff, the first Japanese Chin imported into Japan, became a Champion and Asiatic Champion.

KASUGANO

This line was created in 1962 by Dr Seikoh Yoshida, a veterinary surgeon, and became famous in the Osaka-Kyoto-Kobe area of Japan. It took 15 years to establish the line – studying bloodlines, then researching and experimenting with various matings. Special attention was paid to pre-war lines. Every effort was made to preserve the type, physical constitution and temperament of the breed. It is said that Kasugano dogs are more refined in appearance than other lines. I recently had a letter from Dr Yoshida's son, Seiji Yoshida, who is also a veterinary surgeon. He does not breed or own any Japanese Chins, but possesses some of his father's material about the breed and was kind enough to send the photograph of Tarou Kasugano, unfortunately without further details.

TOKASOW

This line excels in coat, both in quality and length, surpassing other lines in this regard and also in beauty of muzzle. It was established by Masazo Sunaga of Tokyo, a pre-war breeder who was able to retain some original stock for post-war breeding. His most prominent and best dogs were Tsurumaru, Kikumatsu and Saburo. His most famous and widely-used stud dog, Tokasow-Momotaro, lived until he was over ten years of age.

KUMOCHI

The Kumochi line was founded by Ineko Shimogawa of Tokyo. Mrs Shimogawa

Kasugano Taroumaru: One of Dr Seikoh Yoshida's original Kasugano line.

was born in the USA, and returned to Yokohama during her childhood. She began breeding Chins at the age of 16. As a result of the earthquake of 1923, she moved to Kobe where she made the aquaintance of Captain Davidson of S.S. Empress of Russia. He was instrumental in bringing from Vancouver a Japanese Chin dog, Tamachan, which he had bred. Mrs Shimogawa subsequently purchased a bitch, Maru, in Kobe. The Chins bred by Captain Davidson came from Chins he had purchased in Nagasaki. Maru came from Nagoya. Thus the Kumochi line was founded by a bitch from the Nagoya line and a dog who was bred from Nagasaki parentage.

Mrs Shimogawa purchased more bitches from Nagoya and eventually had about 50 Chins. In 1928, Maru sired Kumochi-No-Chiya I, who was exported to Canada in 1931 and became an American Champion. Through this, Mrs Shimogawa became known in the US, and registered her kennel name Kumochi with the American Kennel Club.

In March 1943, she moved to Tokyo, taking with her 12 carefully selected Chins from her 50 dogs. These 12 formed the foundation of her present Kumochi line. During the war, Mrs Shimogawa managed to keep a few dogs, albeit illicitly, from her original breeding of the Nagoya/Nagasaki combination. In olden times in Nagoya, there were two different types of Chin – one with a large head, short nose and rich fluffy coat. The other, known as Kame Chin (literally translated as Tortoise Chin) had a comparatively small head, large nose and was somewhat small in size. The former was thought to be the better quality.

It is interesting to note that the Kumochi line is descended from the ancient Chin indigenous to Nagoya, where it has now ceased to exist. Mrs Shimogawa sold many Chins in the USA in the 1930s and 40s, and in 1965 Mrs Craufurd of the UK's Riu Gu line purchased dogs from her, as did Mrs Brittain.

The Japanese book, *The Chin Dog of Japan,* which was published in the 1960s, has a section entitled 'The Existing Main Lines of the Chin'. Written by breed experts Koichi Uoi, Dr Hideo Wakui and Dr Seikoh Yoshida, and translated by Isao Takayama, the book states that the Kumochi line is one of the five main strains of Japanese Chin in Japan.

Dr Wakui states that the Kumochi Japanese Chin have "characteristics which are perceivable at a glance. They are large in size, well balanced as a whole, distinguished in good appearance, virile and quite noble. The head is large, with an overall roundness, nose short, muzzle broad, eyes large and dark. The coat is long and is good in quality. The only regrettable point is that the size is so large. Conclusion: It is clear that 'Kumochi line' is descended from the ancient Chins indigenous to Nagoya, Japan. Yet, this good-natured ancient Chin has ceased to exisit in Nagoya. It is, therefore, only the 'Kumochi line' that is lineally descended from Nagoya Chin. Preserving one of the traditional Chins in Japan, the 'Kumochi line' is highly valued."

Mrs Shimogawa told Jean Brittain (who met her in Japan and brought two of her dogs back to Britain, one for herself and the other for Mrs Craufurd) that, during the war years, food of all sorts was in short supply and it was strictly forbidden for anyone to keep dogs, with the exception of Airedales and German Shepherds which were used by the police and armed forces. Mrs Shimogawa moved to Tokyo as she was unknown there, and managed to secrete her dogs. By going into the countryside, she was able to buy rice and other foods on the black market, raising the money for these purchases by selling her silk kimonos.

ISHIHARA

The Ishihara line was founded by Kan 'Nosuke Ishihara of Tokyo. Masaya (sired by Tosakow-Momotaro) and Lurihime I produced Kinya and Bohya, both of which Mr Ishihara considered superior to their parents. He therefore proceeded to propagate his own line. These were distinctive by their head type, which was well-balanced and featured impressive, large, dark eyes, a firmly settled short nose and a good muzzle. The reasoning behind this particular expression is explained thus: "The shortening of the nose and muzzle results in the rising of the cheeks, and the condensation thus forced also has a great influence upon the shallowing of the eye-holes, leading to the protrusion of the eyeballs."

I find this particularly interesting. I have never been to Japan, but recall seeing, some 15 or more years ago, my first video of Japanese Chins in Japan. It struck me at that time that many of them had almost 'pop' eyes and that this was visible in a number of photographs of the time. This seems to have almost disappeared now, and most Breed Standards call for a normal, large eye, with of course the "look of astonishment", but not for a protruding eye.

SAGAMINO

The Sagamino line of Tatsuko Fukase of Yokohama is based on the three lines Ishihara, Tokasow and Kumochi. The Sagamino line is unique in this respect, being made up from other main bloodlines. It produces stabilized stock with its own individuality.